the BAD OLD DAYS of MONTANA

the BAD OLD DAYS *of* MONTANA

Untold Stories of the Big Sky State

RANDI SAMUELSON-BROWN

TWODOT®

ESSEX, CONNECTICUT
HELENA, MONTANA

A · TWODOT® · BOOK

An imprint of Globe Pequot, the trade division of
The Rowman & Littlefield Publishing Group, Inc.
4501 Forbes Blvd., Ste. 200
Lanham, MD 20706
www.rowman.com

Distributed by NATIONAL BOOK NETWORK

British Library Cataloguing in Publication Information available

Library of Congress Cataloging-in-Publication Data
Names: Samuelson-Brown, Randi, author.
Title: The bad old days of Montana: untold stories of the Big Sky State /
    Randi Samuelson-Brown.
Other titles: Untold stories of the Big Sky State
Description: Essex, Connecticut: TwoDot, [2023] | Series: The bad old days
    | Includes bibliographical references and index.
Identifiers: LCCN 2023012610 (print) | LCCN 2023012611 (ebook) | ISBN
    9781493067268 (paper) | ISBN 9781493067275 (ebook)
Subjects: LCSH: Montana—History—19th century. | Frontier and pioneer
    life—Montana. | Vigilantes—Montana—History—19th century. |
    Outlaws—Montana—History—19th century.
Classification: LCC F731 .S17 2023 (print) | LCC F731 (ebook) | DDC
    978.6—dc23/eng/20230419
LC record available at https://lccn.loc.gov/2023012610
LC ebook record available at https://lccn.loc.gov/2023012611

He gambled his life to better his condition, but he really didn't believe that his hair might make fringes for a Sioux or a Cheyenne war shirt, or that his mutilated body might be clawed out of a shallow grave by wolves.

—Dorothy M. Johnson, *The Bloody Bozeman*[1]

Contents

Contents

INTRODUCTION

To say that Montana's history is as rugged and unique as the state itself is perhaps nothing more than stating the obvious. Nothing short of the Wild West in all its blazing and infamous glory, Montana to this day retains a frontier character all its own. This book hopes to cast light on some of the murkier stories and the more spurious and shady aspects of

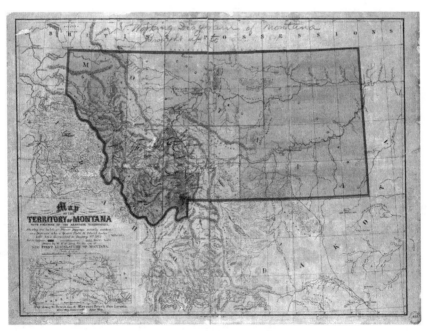

Map of the territory of Montana with portions of the adjoining territories: showing the gulch or placer diggings actually worked and districts where quartz (gold and silver) lodes had been discovered to January 1, 1865.
LIBRARY OF CONGRESS. W. W. (WALTER WASHINGTON) DE LACY, 1819–1892

the collective state history beginning with white settlement. *The Bad Old Days of Montana* is intended as a celebration, and at times a cautionary tale, of just how "bad" conditions and characters used to be.

Structuring Montana's history into a logical sequence, the book begins with the Lewis and Clark expedition. Some of their early camps became the precursors to the so-called forts established by mountain men and the fur trading companies in those same general locations. Beginning roughly in the year 1807 and immediately following the successful return to civilization by the Lewis and Clark expedition, a fascination with the western frontier was born. The possibilities contained within that rugged, untamed territory sparked the collective American imagination like nothing has since the American Revolution. Written about by Meriwether Lewis in his own accounts and taken up and championed by such notables as Washington Irving, the Louisiana Purchase inspired and beckoned. The opportunity promised by westward expansion was not lost on the first American explorers who had already experienced the vastness firsthand. In fact, some of those explorers who accompanied the Lewis and Clark expedition never even made it back to St. Louis before turning around and traveling back to Upper Missouri.

The successful completion of the Lewis and Clark expedition marked the beginning of the American fur trade era. Lasting until approximately 1847, the forts and trading posts established were primarily commercial in nature. However, beginning in the 1850s, the nature of some of the existing trading posts shifted. Along with the decline of the beaver and pelt trade, those remote outposts metamorphized into military establishments. Used for protective purposes, these forts retained a commercial element in many cases: their primary purpose became oversight and protection of the routes and trails for the migration of the American westward expansion.

Upon starting this project, I conducted casual surveys among friends and acquaintances from Montana—especially those whose family lines reached back into the nineteenth-century settlement. Answers to the question "What brought your family to Montana?" were varied. Most answers affirmed what was already suspected and fall into categories closely following the industrial and economic patterns of the state.

People recounted origins in mining, ranching, homesteading, and of becoming supply merchants for the newly settled towns, cities, and camps. Some arrived while working on the railroads and never left. Other responses spoke of troubled lives and the longing for fresh starts in a new wide-open place, which Montana provided. All respondents were proud of their origins, whether their ancestors arrived for the simple one-word answer "gold," or whether they sought a different fortune by establishing a ranch or homestead, working in the copper mines of Butte, or establishing their own business in the sprouting towns and cities.

Some just followed where they felt opportunity and fortune beckoned.

Whatever brought those intrepid people to Montana in the first place, the early statistics are eye-opening. Census data provide a wealth of information, and Montana's first was conducted in 1870.

Ages 5 to 18: 1,134 male / 967 female

Ages 18 to 45: 12,418 male / 6,935 female

Ages 21 and upwards: 13,424 male / 7,450 female[1]

The fact that men outnumbered women substantially between ages eighteen and forty-five would indicate a masculine culture as women were only 36 percent of the population in that age range. The numbers would have been even more skewed in the early 1860s. Such disparity didn't mean refinement was entirely lacking in Montana; it just meant that the population might be considered more rough-and-tumble than other territories or states having an even gender balance.

And a large territory settled primarily by men takes on a certain quality. One can imagine that any "entertainment" might have been of an eyebrow-raising variety. Add alcohol into the mix and things went "off."

THE USE OF DEADLY WEAPONS

We see a poster on our streets warning all persons against the use of deadly weapons, under the pretext of self-defence [sic], or in any other case except for the protection of life and property, and then only as a "last resort," saying that all who violate this will be visited with summary punishment. This notice is signed by the Vigilance Committee. . . . Many persons under the influence of liquor do things which they afterwards regret.

THE MONTANA POST, 1864[2]

ADVENTUROUS CHARACTERS POPULATED THE REGION FROM THE EARLY exploration and trapping days, but when gold was first discovered in the Grasshopper Creek near Bannack in 1862, Montana Territory surged to life with a bang. Miners—traditionally considered a hardworking, hard-drinking lot—flooded into the area. And in no time at all the accompanying offshoots of saloons, dance halls, gambling parlors, and brothels sprung up—all with the intent of separating the miner from his gold in one way or another.

Most citizens at the time carried weapons and weren't afraid to use them. Whiskey-fueled violence came with the territory, arising from disputes for a variety of reasons—some trifling, some serious. In regrettable circumstances, it was the innocent who bore the brunt of this behavior, but often history remains unclear as exactly where to affix blame. Robberies took place with masked men holding up stages transporting fabulous amounts of gold, but the law didn't always prove impartial or trustworthy. Neither did the politics.

Danger could come from many different directions, but placing all of that aside in the quest for gold, people proved willing to take their chances. Because of the amount of mineral riches extracted from the Montana ground (and hence the moniker the Treasure State), pricing was very different in Montana and the West than it was throughout the rest of the country.

For context, the following price valuation chart compares the historic value of a dollar to the 2022 Consumer Price Index (CPI)[3]:

Year	Value of $1 based on 2022 CPI
1860	$35.91
1862	$29.51
1865	$18.28
1870	$22.75
1875	$27.09
1880	$29.22
1885	$30.72
1890	$32.75
1895	$35.48
1900	$35.48
1905	$33.86
1910	$31.37

A shot of rot-gut whiskey that cost twenty-five cents in 1862 would have cost $7.38 in 2022. An encounter with a "frail sister" from a parlor house might cost $15 in 1870, which translates into $341.25. A dress costing $50 in 1900 would cost $1,774 today. Food was scarce, and prices were high—so high in fact that one hundred pounds of flour in Virginia City reportedly cost $110 in 1862. That is the equivalent of $3,246.10 in 2022.

By 1880, the population increased to 39,159, growing to 132,159 in 1890. By 1900 the population was 234,329 as "civilization" took hold, and some of the earlier raucous behavior fell by the wayside.

Where do the "Bad Old Days" come in, and why are Montanans so inordinately proud of them? Because every gunfight, every tall tale, every strike-it-rich story adds to the tapestry of the state. For all the honest hardworking people who raised their families and built schools and churches, it is the improbable tales, horrible storms, vigilante justice, soiled doves, and stolen horses—*and the response* to such challenges—that makes Montana's history stand out as unique, even in the western American frontier. Traces of the past can be found at every turn if they are sought. Suffice to say, Montana was fought over and built by people who took their chances and didn't back down in the face of adversity, whether it be by climate, man, or fortune.

CHAPTER 1

MONTANA IN THE ROUGH BEGINNING

1803–1847

When Napoleon sold the Louisiana Territory to the United States in 1803, the magnitude of land covered was immense, vaguely defined, and absolutely not understood. Consisting of the western half of the Mississippi River's basin, the geography presented an uncharted and great unknown. The newly acquired region stretching west from the Mississippi River and east of the Rocky Mountains would include most of what would later become the state of Montana. In those early days of 1803 and 1804, the territory acquired in the Louisiana Purchase doubled the size of the United States. While a handful of English, French, and Americans had already forged inroads into the region for trapping, the French and the English possessed the upper hand as far as commerce was concerned. Americans had explored along the eastern edges of the former French possession, but settlement crept west slowly. The interior of the Louisiana Territory remained the domain of the Native Americans (or First Peoples) who had inhabited the land for centuries.

Forward-thinking President Thomas Jefferson, with an eye toward expansion, acted as a keen proponent of western settlement. His interest proved both political and practical. Politically, expansion existed as an imperative and desirable goal. Holding to the basic premise that the larger the country, the more power it wielded provided incentive enough. Furthermore, any acquisition of lands that removed territory from potential rival countries created a form of defensive security. It is understandable, with the years of the American Revolution only recently behind them, that the young country felt the need to protect itself against foreign interests and unwanted seizure or colonization. France, a traditional enemy of England, and Spain each had their own colonial aspirations. Jefferson concluded that should war break out between any of those countries, the fledgling United States needed to be prepared to somehow seize the territory west of the Mississippi.

As a practical matter, by the year 1803, the Americans had already started their westward trek and settled upon lands west of that mighty river without any formal directive. Jefferson figured, war or no war, that westward expansion and settlement would continue unabated. What he did not figure on was the slave revolt in Haiti, and Napoleon's dawning realization that a French empire in the Americas might be doomed to failure. The American ambassador to France, Robert R. Livingston, along with James Monroe, were directed at Jefferson's request to purchase New Orleans and the Floridas (at the time Florida was split into an east and west segment). This diplomatic party was authorized to offer $10 million for the land surrounding the strategically important port of New Orleans and the area often referred to as West Florida at the time. When the envoy arrived in Paris, the French did them one better. The French foreign minister offered to sell *all* of the Louisiana territory on April 11, 1803. On April 30, 1803, the Louisiana Purchase Treaty was signed for the bargain price of $15 million or four cents per acre, but that acreage was as yet unknown. As an aside, the Floridas were not acquired with the sale for the simple fact that they belonged to Spain and not to France.

Regardless, under Jefferson's direction, exploration of the new territory was on.

At its heart, the Lewis and Clark expedition was a quest for the Northwest Passage, keeping the fur trade foremost in mind. Europe had developed an insatiable desire for beaver pelts as the latest word in style. Beyond hunting beaver, the Lewis and Clark expedition was a multifaceted endeavor; one mandate of the mission was to scout out the area for commerce and to prepare Native Americans for the upcoming arrival of American traders. Another instruction required a scientific journey, where the explorers were directed to take detailed notes and observations regarding the geography, flora and fauna, the indigenous inhabitants (man and mammal), and the climate. Equally, if perhaps not slightly more pressing, the explorers were instructed to monitor any Canadian intrusions into the fledgling territory. Canada, a full member of the British Empire, was therefore considered an enemy by extension.

Whether referred to as the Lewis and Clark expedition or the Corps of Discovery expedition, a significant portion of their travels and recorded encounters provide context for Montana's later history.

Meriwether Lewis, Jefferson's private secretary, was twenty-nine years old in 1803. While there might have been other men better qualified to act as Jefferson's secretary, Lewis was an excellent fit to lead an expedition. He had fought in the militia during the Whiskey Rebellion, and afterwards had transferred into the regular army. There he met William Clark, the man who would act as his co-commander in the exploration. Clark, at age thirty-three, was the younger brother of George Rogers Clark, the heroic Revolutionary War commander and frontiersman. Together, Lewis and Clark made a formidable team. Clark had more experience with Native Americans, and Lewis acted in the role of recorder and diplomat. Lewis, the more literary of the two, also recorded their findings and all scientific matters. Clark managed most of the logistics including mapping, handling the keel boats, and later the canoes and pirogues. As an added bonus, he turned out to be a talented makeshift doctor. Both men were called "captain," although Clark never received his promised captain's commission. As such he remained, technically, a second lieutenant throughout the expedition. That technicality was not recognized by any of the men in the party, who recognized both leaders as having the same standing. The expedition was a daunting endeavor. Part of the success of the Lewis and Clark expedition was how well both leaders complemented one another and almost always agreed both in public and in private. The educated Lewis was the perfect counterpart to the frontiersman Clark, who reportedly demonstrated greater sympathy and patience with the Indigenous people and was viewed as the better negotiator in such uncharted circumstances.[1]

The expedition set out from St. Louis, Missouri, in mid-May 1804. By October of that year, the party had tested themselves by navigating the Missouri River and managing their encounters with the Arikaras and the Teton Sioux. They traveled upriver far enough to reach the Mandan Villages located north of present-day Bismarck, North Dakota, and sixteen hundred miles upriver from their starting point. The expedition wintered at that location. The band of explorers consisted of twenty-three enlisted men and one slave named York, who was the property of Captain Clark.[2] This band was further divided into three groups led by three sergeants: John Ordway, Patrick Gass, and Nathaniel Pryor. Among the enlisted men were Toussaint Charbonneau and his purchased wife, Sacajawea, a Shoshoni woman who had been kidnapped by the Hidatsa four years earlier. Charbonneau had already traveled widely along the Upper Missouri River, and although Lewis would later call him "a man of no particular merit,"[3] he did speak several Indigenous languages. In addition to these men were two French rivermen and George Douillard, a half Shawnee half French frontiersman who would act as an interpreter.

On April 25 the expedition camped along the Yellowstone River, and from there proceeded to the present-day border of Montana, near the mouth of the Musselshell, where it began to snow. On June 2, the party encountered what would come to be known as the Marias River, a run-off swollen waterway of great size that might have easily been mistaken for the main branch of the Missouri. Later named for Lewis's cousin, Maria Wood, this encounter presented a crucial decision point. There were several forks to the river, and the men spent days examining and exploring each branch to determine the correct passage to the "great falls" described by the Hidatsa. The party's decision proved correct when they arrived at such falls on the Missouri River on June 13, 1805. There they discovered it was not just one waterfall they had to circumnavigate but five. By this time, several members of the expedition had fallen ill, including Sacajawea. The corps would spend one month figuring out how to portage their canoes and equipment the eighteen miles around the formidable barrier. All equipment and supplies had to either be stashed, carried by hand, or transported on makeshift wagons to circumvent the falls. This remarkable feat was fittingly accomplished on Independence Day.

July 4th, Thursday 1805—Towards evening Our officers gave the party the last of the ardent Spirit that we had (excepting a little that they reserved for sickness). . . . We amused ourselves with frolicking, dancing & ca. [sic] until 9 o'clock P. M. [sic] in honor of the day. In the Evening we had a slight shower of Rain, but it soon cleared away, & we had fine weather.[4]

On July 25, 1805, an exhausted Clark and his party reached the Three Forks of the Missouri—the headwater. Lewis's band rejoined them two days later. Naming the three rivers Jefferson, Madison, and Gallatin (then secretary of the treasury), the men headed southwest up the Jefferson River, pulling their canoes while Lewis hurried on ahead, seeking the elusive Shoshoni. They crossed the Continental Divide on August 12 at the Lemhi Pass and traveled downhill where they finally encountered a band of Shoshoni. For their part, the Shoshoni weren't inclined to be trusting of the strangers, wary despite Lewis's goodwill offering of guns.

However, when Clark arrived with his party, which included Sacajawea, the tenor of the meeting changed dramatically. Cameahwait, the chief of the band, was astounded when he and Sacajawea recognized each other. Reunited brother and sister (or perhaps cousins), the expedition was able to trade out weary horses due to this chance encounter. From the Shoshoni, the expedition learned that the path they sought to the Oregon Territory along the Salmon River Country was impassible. The expedition was then guided by an old Shoshoni named Pi-kee queen-ah, but called an Anglicized "Old Toby," into the Bitterroot Valley.

The expedition proceeded over the Lolo Trail—a difficult endeavor in the autumn months. Game proved scarce and the party suffered from hunger. By late September, they dropped into what would later become Idaho and the Clearwater Valley, where friendly Nez Perce provided assistance. The men of the expedition requested their help in constructing boats or canoes, and the tribe kept their horses for them that winter, as the men carried on the expedition down to the sea. They traveled down the Clearwater River, to the Snake, down the Columbia River, and reached their main destination on November 7, 1805.

Near the mouth of the Columbia River, the expedition established an encampment called Fort Clatsop, so named after a local tribe. That winter, by all accounts, proved long and dreary. The men hunted and socialized with the local tribes to pass the time. As would prove so often the case, venereal disease became a problem from these interactions labeled as "socialization."

On March 15, 1806, Lewis wrote:

> *We were visited this afternoon by Delashelwilt, a Chinook Chief, his wife and six women of his nation which the old baud his wife had brought for market. This was the same party that had communicated the venerial [sic] to so many of our party in November last, and of which they have finally recovered. I therefore gave the men a particular charge with rispect [sic] to them which they promised me to observe.[5]*

With the arrival of spring, the Discovery Corps expedition traveled back up the Columbia starting out on the fabulously early seasonal date of March 15, 1806. Upon trading for enough horses, they abandoned their canoes and traveled on horseback back to the Nez Perce where they retrieved their own mounts that had been cared for over the winter months. Of course, snow remained deep on the Bitterroot Mountains, and as a result, their trip over the Lolo Pass was delayed until late June when the mountains cleared. When the route became traversable, and with the assistance of two Nez Perce guides, the expedition crossed over the pass and down into an area they christened "Travelers' Rest." At Travelers' Rest, the men divided into two groups: one led by Clark and the other by Lewis.

Clark's party, accompanied by Sacajawea, met no serious problems other than getting their horses stolen, which was serious enough. On July 15 along the banks of the Yellowstone River, while the men were constructing dugout canoes, a band of Crow stole half of their herd. Clark proceeded downriver with all his party but three, leaving Sergeant Pryor and two men to drive the remaining horses to the Mandan Villages. An embarrassed Sergeant Pryor met up with Clark's main party a few days later on the Missouri River, arriving in hastily constructed skin boats. Much to Pryor's chagrin, the remaining horses under his watch had also been pilfered by the Crow—living up to their reputation as the most skilled horse thieves on the plains. The other side of the coin might have been that Sergeant Pryor and his men were negligent guardsmen, but of course, that was not the recorded version offered at the time.

Loss of horses and embarrassment aside, Lewis's band encountered more serious difficulties. Although his party reached the Great Falls a rapid one week after leaving Travelers' Rest, the trek did not ultimately fare well, despite fast travel and auspicious signs. Taking advantage of their rapid travels (which had taken fifty-eight days on the way out), Lewis took Drouillard to explore the Marias River. The pair made it to the Cut Banks fork, but their "clock" broke, making it impossible for them to determine their exact location. They also encountered a band of Blackfeet, and Lewis agreed to set up camp with them despite having received warnings from the Nez Perce and the Flatheads as to their hostility. In a dangerous and uncustomary lapse of judgment, Lewis told the Blackfeet about bringing arms to their traditional enemies, basically throwing the small party of men square into the status of potential enemies. During that same night, the Blackfeet attempted to seize the explorer's weapons. In the ensuing struggle, Reuben Field knifed and killed one Blackfeet while Lewis shot another dead. The Blackfeet fled, and so did Lewis and his men. It is said that Lewis's party covered an amazing one hundred miles by daylight, when they reached the Missouri River in time to meet the Ordway-Gass party coming downstream from Great Falls.

Apart from the struggle with the Blackfeet and the fact that Lewis got shot in the thigh while hunting, the entire expedition basically came off without incident. The Discovery Corps initiated friendly relations between the Americans and some of the native nations, mapped out an impressive swath of country, laid rest to the notion of the fabled Northwest Passage, and received a hero's welcome upon their return to St. Louis on September 23, 1806. Perhaps more important, in a commercial sense, the expedition challenged the British-Canadian supremacy in the northern regions, declaring the valuable Columbia Valley an American territory. Beyond that, Lewis and Clark spoke with enthusiasm about one valuable commodity—fur. And a few notable members of the expedition-ary forces would return to that same region to become some of the most famous (or infamous) fur traders and mountain men in the West.

A new chapter in American history opened, wide and free.

THE TRADING POSTS AND FORTS

On Lewis and Clark's expedition back to St. Louis between August 3 and August 20 of 1806, it is recorded that they encountered *eleven* separate bands of fur trappers headed up the Missouri River. One of the most elusive and individualistic of American breeds, mountain men (or fur trappers) seldom kept records of their exploits or day-to-day experiences. As such, their individual histories prove scant and largely unverifiable. However, commercial enterprises were much better at keeping accounts, which at least offer a glimpse into the ruggedness and flexibility required to survive out in the wilderness. The fur trading companies established outposts, which at the time were often referred to as forts. Little more than four walls and a roof in many cases, these so-called forts were fre-quently short-lived, staying in business for only a season or two. But those trading posts, trading with either the independent trappers or "company men," opened up commerce in the vast and dangerous wilderness.

Fortunes were waiting to be made by the trapping and peddling of pelts.

As early as 1670, the English Crown chartered the Hudson Bay Company whose original purpose was to seek the elusive Northwest Pas-sage to the Pacific, to settle lands in said region, and to conduct as prof-itable a trade as was available in that territory. In effect, with the creation of the Hudson Bay Company, the race to exploit the Northwest's riches was on. The Hudson Bay Company (HBC) was the only such commer-cial enterprise until 1783, when the North West Company was founded. Established in Montreal after the "Fall of Canada" in 1759 by a group of Scots businessmen, its early history was complicated and convoluted. In short, a notable number of Highlanders and other emigrants from Great Britain settled in the Montreal area and quickly took over what had been previously the French fur trade. Often referred to as "peddlers"—a deri-sive term coined by Hudson Bay employees—the North West Company comprised a group of individuals who pooled their resources to effectively reduce competition among themselves. Beyond that, the North West Company's purpose was also to resist the inland incursions of the HBC. This new upstart took advantage of the existing French infrastructure and hired large numbers of *coureurs du bois* and *voyageurs* as well as taking over the former French fur trading posts in western Canada and northern Ontario. Throughout the late 1760s and into the early 1770s, traders from Montreal and St. Louis, Missouri, absorbed most of the trade west of the Appalachians and east of the Mississippi. The Treaty of Paris was signed on September 3, 1783, effectively creating the current border between Canada and the United States, a divide that gave the Americans access to prime fur-trapping country within the nation's borders.[6] It must be admitted, however, that it took a while for the Americans to gain a true foothold in the fur trading business.

But back to Montana and its wealth of beaver-trapping areas.

In 1804, Charles McKenzie and Francois Antoine Larocque were sent by the North West Company to trade with the Mandan along the Upper Missouri River. Upon their arrival, they discovered four Hudson Bay men established, so they wintered with the nearby Gros Ventres. During this winter, the two men came in close contact with the Lewis and Clark expedition.[7] In 1805, a second North West Company expedition traversed southeastern Montana and reported great quantities of beaver in the Yellowstone River area. These discoveries, however, were not explored further or capitalized upon at that time, likely due to the distances involved.

Meanwhile, John Jacob Astor founded the American Fur Company in the eastern United States. The territory that would become Montana was approached from traders and trappers coming from all directions: Hudson Bay Company and the North West Company pressed down from the north, the American Fur Company trappers came from the east, and immediately following Lewis and Clark's successful return, Spaniard Manuel Lisa established the Missouri Fur Company, which came up from the south.

Manuel Lisa would prove to be one of the more successful traders who made incursions into the territory that would become Montana.

Together with his two partners, William Morrison and Pierre Minard, both from Illinois, Lisa also engaged the services of two veterans of the Lewis and Clark expedition: George Drouillard as interpreter and the legendary John Colter. John Colter had explored the Yellowstone region and perhaps the Absaroka Mountains on his own after the year 1806. In 1807, Lisa founded the first fur trading post in Montana but the second for him personally. Manuel Lisa's first post was located in present-day North Dakota. This Montana establishment provided the model that would soon be followed by others throughout the area. Lisa's post was called by a variety of names, including Fort Manuel, Manuel's Fort, Fort Remon (named for his son), Fort Raymond (the Americanized variation), Fort Manual Lisa, and Lisa's Fort. Completed in November 1807, it was located at the juncture of the Yellowstone and Big Horn Rivers.[8] He went on to establish other forts both in North Dakota and Nebraska. All of Lisa's forts had similar variations of the names listed above.

Fur trapping and trading was big business in the fledgling frontier economy. The various fur trading companies established their forts and outposts in advantageous locations scattered throughout the former Louisiana Territory. These forts formed the bases of their operations, and such establishments signaled the individual company's dominance over a specific territory. Beyond "staking a claim," these forts were often little more than trading posts. And Montana had many such outposts. Categorized by company, year, and outcome, the following grouping provides a snapshot of how business progressed, competing interests, what the outcome of their tenure produced, and highlights the consolidation of the more robust entities, which often lasted into the Plains War years, and occasionally beyond.[9]

Missouri Fur Trading Company (American)

Fort Raymond (1807–1811) near Hysham/Bighorn. The first fort/outpost established by Manuel Lisa, it was also called Fort Remon in honor of Lisa's son. This important post is credited with being the first permanent settlement in Montana. Because of Lisa's obvious friendship with the Crow, this fort was attacked by Blackfeet in either 1810 or 1811. The Blackfeet were traditional enemies of the Crow, provoking such actions.

Three Forks Post (1810) at Three Forks. Alternately referred to as Fort Henry, the fort was built by thirty-two men, including John Colter, Andrew Henry, George Drouillard, and Pierre Menard. The post was abandoned two months after establishment due to Blackfeet hostility. Five trappers were killed by the Blackfeet on April 12, 1810. Eight trappers in total were killed before the post was abandoned, including noted trappers George Drouillard and John Potts.[10]

Fort Benton (1821–1823) on the Yellowstone River near Bighorn. The fort was constructed in the fall of 1821 by Joshua Pitcher and located near Hysham and either nearby or atop of the earlier site of Fort Manuel Lisa. The Missouri Fur Trading company reportedly had about three hundred men in this vicinity. That first year they gathered $25,000 in pelts. Lured by the attractive trapping on Blackfeet land, Jones and Immel led a sizable party to the Jefferson River at the Missouri headwaters. There, in mid-May 1823, they encountered a band of seemingly friendly Blackfeet. Actually, the friendship displayed proved cunning. The Blackfeet secretly raised a large war party and trailed the Americans into Crow territory. Outside of present-day Billings, they ambushed the trappers as they descended through the rim-rocks. Jones and Immel, along with five of the company men, lost their lives. Pelts valued at $15,000 were captured.[11]

American Fur Trading Company (American)
Major Alexander Culbertson, head of the American Fur Trading Company, had a wife who was of the Blackfeet Nation named Natawista, or Medicine Snake Woman. Their union facilitated relations with the Blackfeet, as Natawista assisted in negotiations and interpretations.[12]

Fort Piegan (1831–1832) Loma. Established in October 1831, this outpost is credited with being the first successful venture among the Blackfeet. At the time, it consisted of three log buildings surrounded by a 25-foot palisade (wooden stockade wall). It was abandoned in 1832.

Fort Cass (1832–1835) two miles east of present-day Custer. Built by Samuel Tullock. This 130-foot-square cottonwood fort included two

Fort Benton
LIBRARY OF CONGRESS

blockhouses (defensive structures with loopholes for firing). It was also known as Samuel Tulloch's Fort.

Fort McKenzie (1832–1844) near Loma. Built on the north bank of the Missouri River, fourteen miles upriver from Fort Benton, this post is also referred to as the second Fort Piegan. Operated by David Mitchell, it was located about six miles above the mouth of the Marias River and was constructed as a 1,420-foot quadrangular stockade. It was abandoned in 1844 and burned by the company, resulting in the nickname Fort Brulee, which translates to "burned fort." At some point (perhaps August 28, 1833[13]) a band of Piegan (Blackfeet) traders were killed outside the fort by a reported six thousand Assiniboine and Cree before the Americans could open the gate. This renewed the hostilities between the Blackfeet and the Americans. Another episode occurred in 1843 when two trappers named F. A. Chardon and Alexander Harvey sought revenge because they believed members of the Blackfeet tribe had killed Chardon's slave, whose name has been lost to history. In retaliation, the trappers used a concealed cannon, which they fired at a band of Blackfeet, killing twenty-one and wounding others. To make matters worse, the trappers killed the wounded and scalped the bodies. The fort was abandoned in 1844 due to fear of reprisals. Indeed, the Blackfeet burned the remaining structures to the ground thereafter.[14]

Fort Jackson (1833–1834) near Park Grove. Established December 1833 by Frances Chardon, it was abandoned the following year.

Fort Assiniboine (1834–1836) near Poplar. Its exact location is unknown, simply noted as being on the Montana/North Dakota border, north of Fort Union. This is where the steamer *Assiniboine* ran aground and was forced to remain for the winter. Reportedly the post sprang up around the stranded ship as a result.

Fort Van Buren (1835–1842) near Cartersville and east of Forsyth, along the Rosebud. Built by Samuel Tullock to replace Fort Cass, this fort was abandoned and burned by Charles Larpenteur in 1842 when the American Fur Trading Company declared bankruptcy and went out of business.

Fort F. A. Chardon (1844–1845) near Everson. Built by Frances Chardon and Alexander Harvey, the fort was abandoned by Major Alexander Culbertson, the head of the American Fur Trading Company, in 1845.

Fort Lewis (1846–1847) originally established eighteen miles northeast of Fort Benton. Also known as Fort of the Blackfeet, it was dismantled and reassembled at the site of Fort Benton due to Blackfeet request. This was accomplished by floating the logs downriver.

Fort Benton (1847–1881) originally built as Fort Clay. It was located on the Missouri River and built for the Blackfeet trade. This fort played an important and ongoing role in Montana's history.

Harvey Primeau and Company
Fort Campbell (1845–1860) near Fort Benton. This *opposition* trading post (opposition to the American Fur Trading Company) was built by

Alexander Harvey. It was located where Fort Benton's adobe structures now stand.

Union Fur Company
Fort Cotton or Fort Cotton Bottoms (late 1842, or early 1843; abandoned 1844). Little is known about this fort located ten miles southwest of Fort Benton. Some sources credit the American Fur Company with establishing this post.

North West Company (Canadian)
Kootenai Post (1808) Rexford. Built by David Thompson, a former Hudson Bay employee and noted geographer and surveyor. It was a short-lived post.

Kootenai Post (1808–1809) Libby. Originally built by Finan McDonald, David Thompson's lieutenant. Later the post was relocated three miles upstream. Established profitable and friendly trade with the Kutenai and Salish tribes.

Saleesh House (1809–1810, 1811–1813) Thompson Falls. Built by David Thompson whose legacy had a firm foothold in the region and who left an amazingly accurate mapping of the Missoula area and surrounding countryside. It is believed Thompson left that post in 1811, after which a group of Kootenai took up residence. The Kootenai were attacked by a group of Piegans. Jon McTavish had the post rebuilt and reopened in December 1811.

Kootenai Post (1811–1812) Jennings. It was located along the Fisher River in the present-day town of Jennings.

Kootenai Post (1821–1824, 1829–unknown) near Libby. Located above the Kootenai Falls, the post was taken over by the Hudson Bay Company shortly after construction.

Hudson Bay Company (British)
Fort Joseph Howes / Howes House (1810–1811) Flathead Valley, exact location unknown. It was built by Joseph Howes.

Flathead Post (1823–1847) Eddy. Established by Alexander Ross, and possibly moved several times. Some sources list this installation as a North West Company post. In 1846 it was moved to Charlo and renamed Post Connah.[15]

Kootenai Post (1846–1860) Rexford. Also called Fort Kootenai and Linklater's Post (after 1852). After the 49th Parallel was surveyed, the post moved into Canada and later was replaced by Fort Steele, British Columbia.[16]

Flathead Post / Fort Connah (1846–1872) St. Ignatius, six miles south of Ronan. The last Hudson Bay outpost constructed in the United States. Started by David Thompson and known as Salish House, it was constructed by Neil McArthur and Angus McDonald in 1847. This is the last of HBC's major posts and was the company's primary post in Montana.[17]

Pacific Fur Company
Flathead Post (1812–1813) Noxon. Built by Alexander Ross and transferred to the North West Company in November 1813 before closing.

The "opening" of the western United States was widely influenced by fur companies in their quest for riches. The government, although interested in the commercial endeavors, was far more concerned with competing national interests, otherwise known as politics. The western expansion fostered advancements in trading practices with the Native Americans while establishing supply networks. While the ins and outs of the individual fur companies' histories and motivations reflect complex aims and aspirations, the individual companies reflected the nationalist and economic factors at play. Lured by the temptation of fortunes to be made, the fur companies invested considerable time and energy (not to mention money) promoting and funding their remote outposts, many of which were located in what would become the Montana Territory. Those outposts/trading posts inserted a rough organization in the wilderness. Those outposts or forts established tenuous settlements where the adventurous and hardy might try their luck at commerce and survival.

Competition characterized the race to dominate the region. Britain, France, and the relatively young United States each vied for supremacy. In direct competition with each other, companies closely tied to nationalistic interests each sought to locate and establish operations in the most profitable locations possible. Conflicts ensued. In the case of the territory that would become Montana, John Astor's American Fur Trading Company proved the emergent force. Second in prominence in the region was the North West Company, followed by the Hudson Bay Company, whose territory covered part of what is now the western reaches of Montana. As the name clearly states, John Astor's *American* Fur Trading Company was an American pursuit, the North West Company was Canadian, and the Hudson Bay Company was English.

Each of the three prominent companies carried and demonstrated vested national interests coupled with their trading ventures. In 1846, the HBC and the American Fur Company signed a treaty that essentially agreed each enterprise would stay out of the other's territory.[18] It is impossible to know how closely that agreement was followed by the men in their pursuit of beaver.

What few might have realized in the first half of the nineteenth century was that the days of the beaver were numbered. What they also didn't know was that there were other riches to harvest and other fortunes to be made. But for a brief golden age, the mountain men embodied the yearnings of a young American nation as they reaped their reward in the wilderness.

CHAPTER 2

THE MOUNTAIN MEN
AND TRAPPERS

1815–1840

*It is difficult to do justice to the courage, fortitude, and perseverance
of the pioneers of the fur trade, who conducted these early expeditions,
and first broke their way through a wilderness where every thing was
calculated to deter and dismay them. . . . They knew nothing of the
country beyond the verge of their horizon, and had to gather information as they wandered. . . . In vain may the most cruel and vigilant
savages beset his path; in vain may rocks, and precipices, and wintry
torrents oppose his progress; let but a single track of a beaver meet his
eye, and he forgets all dangers and defies all difficulties.*
—WASHINGTON IRVING, 1837[1]

WRITERS LIKE WASHINGTON IRVING PORTRAYED AN IDEALIZED EXIS-
tence, but frontier explorer, mountain man, and entrepreneur General
Thomas James of the Three Forks Post, also known as Fort Henry,
recorded the reality a bit differently. His contemporaneous account dwelt
more on practicalities and highlighted factions and differences between
the trappers, companies, and hierarchies.

*I enlisted in this expedition, which was raised for trading with the
Indians and trapping for beaver on the head waters of the Missouri*

*and Columbia rivers. The whole party, at starting, consisted of 350
men, of whom about one half were Americans and the remainder
Canadian Frenchmen and Creoles of Kaskaskia, St. Louis and other
places. The French were all veteran voyageurs, thoroughly inured to
boating and trapping. Manuel Liza, called by the men "Esaw" had
enlisted many of them . . . by the year. . . .* [2]

*The French hands were much better treated on all occasions than
the Americans. The former were employed for a long period at stated
wages and were accustomed to such service and such men as those in
command of them, while we were private adventurers for our own benefit, as well as that of the company, who regarded us with suspicion and
distrust. Many Americans on the passage up the river, disgusted with
the treatment they received, fell off in small companies and went back.* [3]

In these passages, James refers to the different categories of trappers and
the distinctions as to how they made their money. As James explains,
there were the individual (or private trappers) and the "company men."
While the image of a lone mountain man traversing the wilderness is
what remains etched in historical memory, in practice not all mountain
men pursued a solitary path. The trappers had the option to join forces
with a specific company or operation, thus becoming employees or company men of those specific institutions. Others who eschewed such alliances were known at the time as "independent" or "free men." Of course,
there were pros and cons to each situation.

Company men were essentially employees of a specific concern.
Often, they received their "outfit"—guns, provisions, traps, and trading
supplies—as a condition of their labor or employment. Because of this
initial outlay by, in essence, their employer, such positions did not pay
as handsomely as what an independent trapper who furnished his outfit
at his own expense could earn. In both instances, men were paid by the
number of pelts they brought in; however, for the company men, the
prices were capped at the prevailing company rates. In addition to the
capped bounties or prices, the company would tell the men where to hunt
and trap. Beyond following such directions, employees were required to
perform other chores as deemed necessary, which could include such

Piegan Indians standing and on horseback in front of a large number of tipis at an encampment on the Musselshell River, Montana, with bluffs in the background, near Fort McKenzie.
LIBRARY OF CONGRESS. PUBLISHED BY DANIEL RICE & JAMES G. CLARK, PHILA., [1842]

tasks as cutting trees, building structures, and performing any number of maintenance duties.

As James lamented,

> *We Americans were all private adventurers, each with his own hook, and were led into the enterprise by the promises of the company, who agreed to subsist us to the trapping grounds, we helping to navigate the boats, and on our arrival there they were to furnish us each with a rifle and sufficient ammunition, six good beaver traps and also four men of their hired French, to be under our individual commands for a period of three years. By the terms of the contract each of us was to divide one-fourth of the profits of our joint labor with the four men thus appointed to us.*[4]

In the instance of James, he and his fellow Americans provided their labor in exchange for transportation into the wilderness. Upon reaching a predetermined destination, such laborers would receive consideration in trade for the work performed. Although James described himself and the other Americans as "private adventurers," they had, in practice, transformed into a version of company men complete with contract.

The Hudson Bay Company often sent out its company trappers in "brigades" of forty to sixty men, a practice started in 1818 and led by Donald McKenzie. The large numbers of men assured comparative safety of numbers in hostile and unknown territories. In 1824, the recorded tally from the brigade led by Alexander Ross was an impressive five thousand pelts. But mountain men were mountain men, whether company or free, and their behavior could be as violent and as rough as the surrounding terrain. For the next six years, HBC brigades were led by Peter Skene Ogden, a shrewd man known for his toughness and even viciousness. Legends of his temper abound, including one reported incident where in a particular fit of anger he ordered one of his men to climb a tree and then set the tree afire from below. He then forced the man to climb back down through the flames.[5] It is unclear what sparked such a violent reaction. One can only hope that such severe conduct was precipitated by a transgression of a very serious nature.

Manuel Lisa, one of the founders of the Missouri Fur Company, has more of a complete history. Born in New Orleans in 1772 and a man of ambition, he married a widow named Polly Charles Chew by 1796 and obtained a land grant in Missouri from Spanish officials for the purpose of agriculture in 1799/1800. He moved with his wife to St. Louis, where they lived with three children, whose names are unknown. It is also unknown whether some, or all, of the children were from Polly's first marriage. The family stayed behind in civilization while Lisa traveled into the vast wilderness. After founding Fort Lisa in 1813, Lisa was appointed as a US Indian Agent for the Missouri Territory. Like many other mountain men, he established a second family in addition to the one he left behind. In 1814 he married Mitane, a daughter of Big Elk, chief of the Omaha. The marriage was viewed as a strategic alliance that yielded two children. It was likely that Lisa's family back in St. Louis remained unaware of this.

Polly Chew Lisa died in 1817. Lisa married again in 1819, to another widow named Mary Hempstead Keeney. He took this newest wife with him on an expedition out to Fort Lisa in Nebraska, where they wintered. He tried to gain custody of his two children with Mitane, who had allowed their daughter Rosalie to attend Catholic school in St. Louis but refused to relinquish her son. Lisa made provisions for all his children upon his death, which occurred in 1820.

What this story illustrates is that mountain men often established families and tribal alliances. It is unclear how the families left behind in "the States" viewed their husbands' second Native unions, if they were even known. In some cases, these marriages or alliances were love matches, establishing an exclusive commitment. Other adventurers, with less admirable motives, pursued tribal marriages for convenience, power, or economic reward.

Married or single, the independent or free men worked for themselves, without any assistance such as the company men enjoyed. Supplying their own traps, guns, provisions, and trade goods, these independent men were able to command higher prices (or at least the prevailing market rate) for the pelts they brought in for trade. Free trappers came in two categories. The first type was a company outfitted man who received no wage. In return for his outfit, he was required to sell his pelts to his employers. It stands to reason that the prices paid were depressed as a result of the "stake" or original investment. The truly free or independent trappers were beholden to no one and did as they pleased. They trapped where they wanted, lived as they chose, and answered to no one other than their own conscience and desires. These men, free to negotiate their own terms, usually commanded higher prices for their pelts.

The monetary reward or success depended largely upon the risks a trapper was willing to take. The same could often be said for the individual forts or outposts.

In either situation, company or free, the mountain men traded with the Native peoples, as did the individual forts and outposts. An often-overlooked fact is that the tribes provided a larger percentage of the pelts than did the mountain men or trappers. Individuals and outposts formed alliances with specific Indian tribes in their immediate regions for that reason. The Hudson Bay Company, because of decent trading practices, held the loyalty of the western Montana tribes. The American Fur Trading Company focused their attention upon the Blackfeet. The Missouri Fur Trading Company was partial to the Crow, and the North West Company welcomed the Kootenai.

Individual histories of the majority of mountain men have faded and disappeared into the shadows of time—largely unknown and widely undocumented. Those few who became leaders and legends may have a bit more written about them due to their prominence. It was the rare mountain man who kept a journal or diary, but those that did survive have often been published. These personal accounts provide insights into the workings and tribulations of lives carved out of the wilderness.

A roughly individualistic breed, mountain men proved rugged, self-sufficient, and solitary but possessed certain common traits. They all left the white civilization and struck out deep into Native territory, many adopting at least part of the lifestyle of the nearby tribes, including marriages, family, and kin. Some of these familial alliances provided a great boon to trade success, such as the match between Fort Benton founder Alexander Culbertson and his Blackfeet wife, Natawista Ixsana. By all accounts, their marriage began as a highly successful pairing and Natawista was described by none other than John James Audubon as "handsome, really courteous and refined."[6] The Culbertson's union produced five children, who received superior educations. Later the family would move to Illinois, where Natawista and Alexander's marriage was formalized in a Catholic ceremony. Alas, life did not prove entirely kind to the family. Having amassed a large fortune, a series of bad investments resulted in bankruptcy and a return west in 1868. In the year 1870, for reasons unknown, Natawista returned to the Blackfeet and Alexander died at the home of his daughter and son-in-law George H. Roberts, the attorney general of Nebraska.

Some of the marriages were business arrangements between the white trappers and their Native wives. Critical accounts often describe such unions as little more than slavery for the women who were sold or traded by male relatives for gain. For a time, this blending of the two cultures produced a measure of understanding and alliance as relationships were struck up and built. However, a clash of cultures loomed on the horizon, a clash that would seriously compromise the autonomy and survival of the tribes in the future. But in those early days of the nineteenth century, few could have foreseen the pending devastation.

Trappers and mountain men with their wives and families, if they had them, fanned out in the remotest regions. What was known as mountain men's Rendezvous provided an occasion for the people to come together from far and wide. Meaning "to meet at an agreed time or place," such gatherings began in 1825 and ended in 1840; however, none are believed to have taken place in Montana. Founded by William Henry Ashley, co-owner of the Rocky Mountain Fur Company, these Rendezvous were held largely in the Wyoming region with a couple taking place in Utah. Drawing mountain men from all over the region, the main purpose of the gathering was for the host company to purchase pelts, and hopefully sell plenty of goods to the men to reoutfit them for the winter. The men, in all practicality, needed the business aspect of the Rendezvous, but there is little doubt that fun and comradery were the main draw. Accounts emphasize the heavy drinking and overall general conviviality and debauchery that such gatherings inspired. Of course, participation in the varied activities was left up to the individual temperaments of the mountain men involved.

Statistically, it is *believed* that the actual number of mountain men or fur traders was fairly small; a general consensus puts the number at around three thousand such individuals engaged in trapping for profit between 1825 and 1840. The men, by most accounts, struck out west in their late teens and twenties. The majority were white, but there are accounts of black and mixed-blood trappers (often descendants of French-Canadian fathers and Native mothers). The stories behind the individual trappers are likely as varied and unique as the individuals themselves; however, it seems reasonable to assume that those who ultimately became mountain men didn't originate from cities. Most were probably raised in rural areas, possessing a practical understanding of survival on the frontier, skilled in the use of guns, horses, and hunting. If sons of the eastern cities hazarded the mountains, they would have had much to learn along the way, but that's not to say that it couldn't be done.[7]

One of the hardest aspects to reconcile to is an almost certain lonely death. It's hard to pinpoint how many lost their lives to attacks by local tribes or grizzly encounters, or succumbed to death due to injury, illness, accident, or old age. One estimate is that between the years 1822–1829, seventy mountain men died of "unnatural" causes. Another source estimates that one mountain man died per week, and yet another reckoned that the men killed by Native tribes ran from about ten to twenty per year, from the years 1825 to 1830.[8] Therefore, if three thousand men could be designated as "mountain men" and one does the math based upon those estimates, the death rate per year comes out to around 10 percent from violent causes, and the statistic of "one mountain man died per week" returns a mortality rate of about 26 percent per year. It's difficult to estimate whether experience increased the odds of survival by individual man, but it would seem probable. On the balancing side, however, is the fact that each dangerous encounter would take its toll—especially attacks by Indigenous fighters where the best odds would be 50–50 based on single, hand-to-hand encounters.

Natural causes of death must have included illness and old age, statistics of which are unknown.

Despite those risks, mountain men, as a group, captured the admiration of Americans. Signaling a new era in American expansion, the general public longed to read about their daring exploits in the rugged West. Contemporaries of the time wrote enthusiastically of this new breed of frontiersmen, including Washington Irving in *The Adventures of Captain Bonneville, or, Scenes Beyond the Rocky Mountains of the Far West*, first published in 1837.

That same year of 1837, however, marked one of the first unintended clashes of the cultures, and this came against an invisible foe. The SS *St. Peters*, an American Fur Company steamboat, made its way carrying trade goods to the Upper Missouri River with an unintended and deadly passenger—smallpox. While company personnel reportedly tried to inoculate Native Americans living near Fort Union, they fled and scattered, carrying the disease along with them. The smallpox spread into western Montana and up into Canada, carrying death in its wake. At the Missouri headwaters, Alexander Cuthbertson arrived at a large Blackfeet camp and found only two survivors:

"[H]undreds of decaying forms of human beings, horses, and dogs lay everywhere, scattered among the lodges." The epidemic continued until the winter snows fell, killing two-thirds of the Blackfeet, half of the Assiniboine and Arikara, one-third of the Crow, and one-quarter of the Pawnee.[9]

Tragically, this was a scenario that would repeat with time.

THE ESSENCE OF LEGEND

Out of legends and wildly romantic frontier visions sprang the likes of John Colter, Jim Bridger, Hugh Glass, and George Drouillard—real, living men who embodied the frontier spirit of the time. John Colter is widely credited with discovering the region of the Yellowstone. Called "Colter's Hell" at the time, the mountain man had been sent out into the wilderness by Manuel Lisa in the rough winter of 1807–1808. Because of the severity of the weather, the intent was for Colter to bring the Native tribes back to the fort to trade. At the time, Colter made no record of his journey, but two years later William Clark wrote an account based upon Colter's recollections. Due to the peculiarities of the Yellowstone landscape, Colter was widely accused of exaggerating, if not outright lying, about his experiences. Today, however, it is generally accepted that Colter was the first white man to explore the Yellowstone region and the area near present-day Cody, Wyoming.

Colter is also known for joining up with John Potts, another member of the Lewis and Clark expedition, near Three Forks, Montana, in 1808. Setting out from Fort Raymond to negotiate trade deals with various tribes, Colter and Potts were accompanied by eight hundred Flathead and Crow. They ran across a huge party of Blackfeet, reportedly numbering fifteen hundred, and a fight ensued. While the Colter/Potts/Flathead/Crow contingent proved successful, Colter suffered a leg wound in the exchange—either by arrow or gunshot. Whatever the case, Colter and Potts fortunately made it back to Fort Raymond and comparative safety.

In 1809 Colter and Potts again ventured forth, and again they ran into Blackfeet. The men were paddling up the Jefferson River, and the Blackfeet located on the banks of the river challenged them. The Blackfeet demanded the men come ashore. Colter acquiesced, and he was disarmed and stripped naked. Potts refused to cooperate, and a shot was fired from the bank, wounding him. Potts returned fire and was subsequently shot numerous times and died from his wounds.

Thus, begins one of the most recognized mountain men tales.

The Blackfeet held council and Colter, still naked, was told to run. A strong runner, he took off, without shoes, followed by a pack of young Blackfeet braves. Colter outran most of his would-be assailants but one. According to John Bradbury in 1817:

> *Again, he turned his head and saw the [brave] not twenty yards from him. Determined if possible to avoid the expected blow, he suddenly stopped, turned round, and spread out his arms. The Indian, surprised by the suddenness of the action, and perhaps at the bloody appearance of Colter, also attempted to stop; but exhausted with running, he fell whilst endeavouring to throw his spear, which stuck in the ground, and broke in his hand. Colter instantly snatched up the pointed part, with which he pinned him to the earth, and then continued his flight.[10]*

As the story goes, the mountain man snatched up a blanket from the dead brave and made his way another five miles to where he hid along the Madison River. Hiding in beaver lodges when possible, Colter walked at night and hid during the day. He walked eleven days to make it back to Manuel Lisa's fort, arriving emaciated. In 1810 he helped build two more forts in the region, but at the end of that year returned to St. Louis. Colter settled down and married in Sullen Springs, Missouri, and died of jaundice in 1813.

Hugh Glass, another well-known mountain man, was most noted for his encounter with a grizzly and of being left for dead. Before that happened, however, Glass joined Gen. William Ashley's 1823 expedition (the first being held in 1822). They met up with returning members of the 1822 party, and the combined companies were attacked by the Arikara. Glass was shot in the leg during that skirmish but survived. In a gesture of kindness, he wrote home to the parents of John S. Gardiner, who did not survive the encounter. Glass was widely believed to be illiterate, and someone else might have penned the correspondence with its eccentric spelling, but Glass is credited with the content.

Dr Sir: My painfull duty it is to tell you of the deth of yr son wh befell at the hands of the Indians 2d June in the early morning. He died a little while after he was shot and asked me to inform you of his sad fate.

We brought him to the ship when he soon died. Mr. Smith a young man of our company made a powerful prayr wh moved us all greatly and I am persuaded John died in peace. His body we buried with others near this camp and marked the grave with a log. His things we will send to you. The [Arikara] are greatly treacherous.

We traded with them as friends but after a great storm of rain and thunder they came at us before light and many were hurt. I myself was shot in the leg. Master Ashley is bound to stay in these parts till the traitors are rightly punished. Yr Obt Svt Hugh Glass.[11]

In late August or early September 1823, Glass acted as a hunter for Major Andrew Henry's exploration party of the Rocky Mountain Fur Company up in the Grand River Valley. Heading toward the Yellowstone River, Glass was sent ahead to find food. Unfortunately, he encountered a female grizzly with her two cubs and ended up badly mauled in the exchange. The grizzly grabbed him by the neck and shoulder, flinging him into the air. Landing upon the ground, the wounded mountain man tried to escape, but the grizzly attacked again, this time leaving deep gashes in his left arm and the back of his head. Glass's hunting partner heard the commotion and ran to his aid. One of the cubs gave chase, but Glass's hunting partner managed to kill it. The rest of the Henry party caught up and succeeded in killing the grizzly, who was standing over Glass apparently ready to finish him off.

Due to the severity of his wounds, the rest of his party figured the mountain man would never survive the night. However, the next morning came and Glass remained very much alive. Because all of the men were still in hostile Native territory, Major Henry determined the best course of action was to keep moving; so a litter was built to carry the wounded trapper.

The going was slow and most likely painful.

Worse, the slow pace put the other men at risk as well. Major Henry offered $80 to any two men who would stay behind to bury Glass when he finally died; the offer was accepted by an older man named John Fitzgerald and a younger man referred to as "Bridges." Bridges is now thought to be Jim Bridger, whose age coincided. Hugh Glass was still alive five days after the main party departed. Growing uneasy and perhaps feeling like sitting ducks, the two men absconded with Glass's rifle and left him to die. Summonsing his strength and realizing that he had been abandoned, Glass crawled toward the Missouri River, progress slow and difficult. He subsisted on whatever food he could find. As the story goes, he was driven forward by an instinct of survival and an overwhelming desire for revenge.

By mid-October 1823, Glass reached Fort Kiowa, also known as Fort Lookout or Fort Brasseau. The fort was between 250 miles to 350 miles from where he was abandoned—the distance dependent upon the version of the account consulted. In his desire for revenge, it is said that Glass somehow decided that the youthful Bridger was innocent of the misdeed and the blame fell to the older man. One version has Glass tracking Fitzgerald down to a cavalry outpost where the man was enlisted. There, Glass he wasn't allowed to shoot a soldier, but the commanding officer made Fitzgerald give Glass his rifle back.

In 1833, Glass was in residence in Fort Cass, sixty miles east of Billings. Fort Cass was also often referred to as Samuel Tulloch's Fort. There are conflicting accounts of his death, but likely he was killed with two fellow trappers along the Yellowstone River. Recent research names those two men as Hilain Menard and Colin Rose.[12] Another version has Glass dying in the state of Missouri.

A lesser known but equally fascinating tale belongs to George Drouillard. A member of the Lewis and Clark expedition, Drouillard was referred to as "Drewyer" in their journals. Born of a French father and a Shawnee mother, Drouillard acted as a French interpreter for the expedition as well as a translator of Indigenous languages. Over time, and as Blackfeet violence escalated, the trappers at Menard and Henry's post at Three Forks came under attack. On April 12, 1810, five of the company's trappers were killed. Most of the other trappers remained in the relative safety of the post, only sending out small bands to tend the traps as required. According to General Thomas James of the Missouri Fur Company,

> *[A] Shawnee half-breed named Druyer [Drouillard] . . . went up the river one day and set his traps about a mile from the camp. In the morning he returned alone and brought back six beavers. I warned him of the danger. "I am too much of an Indian to be caught by Indians," said he. On the next day he repeated the adventure and returned with the product of his traps, saying, "this is the way to catch beaver." . . . [T]wo other Shaw-nees [sic] left us against our advice, to kill deer. We started forward as a company and soon found the dead . . . pierced with lances, arrows and bullets and lying near each other. Further on, about one hundred and fifty yards, Druyer and his horse lay dead, the former mangled in a horrible manner; his head . . . cut off, his entrails torn out. And his body hacked to pieces. We saw from the marks on the ground that he must have fought in a circle on horseback, and probably killed some of his enemies."[13]*

One of the most remarkable accounts of a fur trader, scout, and a self-proclaimed chief of the Crow was James Beckwourth—a man who was not above exaggeration. Regaling the reader with accounts of skirmishes, battles, trapping, and daring-do, some of the tales loom large—almost landing squarely into the tall-tale category. However, Beckwourth provides an insight into the hardships of life as a trapper, and valuable insights into life among the Crow. It is Beckwourth who admits to taking scalps—the same as tribal warriors.

Beckwourth was born April 6, 1798, to a white Virginia planter named Sir Jennings Beckwith and a slave woman. There is no account explaining the reason behind changing his last name from Beckwith to Beckwourth: however, upon moving to St. Louis with his father and siblings, he received his manumission. Beckwourth was educated and trained as a blacksmith. In 1823 he signed up as a groom on a fur trading expedition; one year later he joined the Rocky Mountain Fur Company. Married to Crow women several times over, Beckwourth seemed to long for his friends back in St. Louis and returned to that city in 1837 after his contract was not renewed by the American Fur Company. Beckwourth changed fur companies frequently. Nevertheless, he continued to be drawn to the Crow and the western frontier.

Beckwourth loomed large in the West for many years to come, as an explorer, guide, and soldier. He continued to play a prominent role in the West even after the demand for beaver pelts ended. He died in Denver sometime in 1866 or 1867.

When the trade in beaver pelts ended, it took with it one of the mountain men's primary sources of income. There are multiple reasons for the decline in the beaver pelt trade—including overtrapping and the whims of fashion. Beaver was replaced by silk and nutria, a less-expensive South American pelt also suitable for felting. Faced with competition from these new and preferred materials, the price of beaver pelts fell in the panic of 1837. The prices might fluctuate, but pelts brought in only about four dollars each. The predictions that the beaver would become extinct started as early as 1826, and in the 1830s that trend accelerated. By the 1840s most of the mountain men would be gone, and for a few years not much happened in the Montana Territory that was recognized by the rest of the States. Some of the trading forts would remain and become reestablished as US Army outposts. The town of Fort Benton would remain, ready to welcome the next influx of travelers and explorers. And those travelers would come. This time they were looking for a different type of riches. This time they came looking for gold.

CHAPTER 3

GOLD IN 1862

The Birth of Bannack

MONTANA'S RUSH CAME ON THE HEELS OF THE CALIFORNIA, NEVADA, and Colorado gold strikes, as the "easy" gold had been gathered and faced decline when pickings were slim. The prospectors, arriving by steamboat at Fort Benton or overland, struck out toward the western slope of the "Idaho" Rockies where gold discoveries had been reported. John White, a member of one Colorado-based band, found gold along the banks of Grasshopper Creek in July 1862, and the town of Bannock sprang up almost immediately thereafter. At the time, White called the diggings "grasshopper" due to the profusion of the insects swarming the area. Word got out as it tended to do. The population was estimated at four hundred that fall but climbed to three thousand inhabitants during the spring of 1863. At some point, the name switched from Grasshopper Diggings to Bannock. The post office was established on November 21, 1863, when the *o* in the camp's new name was inadvertently read as an *a*, and the unusual spelling was born.[1]

Montana's gold strikes were placer deposits, known as "poor man's diggings," meaning no special skill was required to collect the scattered gold. Placer was surface gold in active or dried-up riverbeds where the particulate mineral was once deposited by water or glacial activity as flakes, dust, or nuggets. The newfound deposits attracted the get-rich-quick types, armed with little more than shovels and gung ho to harvest what they expected would prove easy riches.

Montana Mine. Eight men, holding pickaxes and shovels, standing in front of the entrance to the mine.
LIBRARY OF CONGRESS. JOHN C. H. GRABILL, 1889

As was the nature of gold strikes, word of the discoveries in Montana (known at the time as Idaho Territory) traveled like lightning. What is interesting about all of this gold and mining activity was the *response* to the riches, rather than the riches themselves. It is no secret that gold lures an array of treasure seekers. It attracts the industrious, the fool-hardy, the lazy, and the shiftless. People who struck out for adventure, or were hell-bent on obtaining so-called easy money, all blew through the territory. The women who "mined the miners" arrived, and so did the provisioners. It was those blacksmiths, shopkeepers, haulers, and the like who, in hindsight, followed the surest path to financial success. None of these developments were unique to the Montana Territory, but Montana's response to the logistics of northern remoteness created a culture all its own.

While other western territories may have had problems with robberies, claim jumping, sluice box raiders and their ilk, miner's courts were swiftly established. Those courts issued a type of community law that dealt with transgressions in an effective and hopefully even hand. Although many of Montana's early miners got their start in California or in the later Pike's Peak rush, the methods established in those states failed to take strong hold in Montana for unknown reasons. In fact, miner's law proved effective in Colorado until formalized law and statues were established. Of course, transgressions transpired, but relatively few murders and thefts occurred, or at least few were recorded. Not so in Montana. Montana belonged in the "shoot 'em down or hang 'em up" variety. If contemporary accounts are to be believed, the violence in Montana far outpaced anything experienced elsewhere.

But first, some background on what led up to Montana's distinctive response to extremely portable riches, meaning gold, and the attention such portable riches create. By 1866 the Montana Territory had catapulted to the second largest gold-producing region in the United States—its production amounts surpassed only by California. At that time, Montana's population stood at 28,000 but declined later during that decade.[2] Many of Montana's population were transient, chasing the next strike in what they termed "stampeding." Single men proved far more interested in pursuing riches than in building towns, or even establishing suitable living accommodations. They slept in bedrolls—tents if they had them—in wagon beds or underneath, or they constructed rough brush wickiups. In any case, initially they were unwilling to take the time to establish living quarters. Their mining considerations held sway, especially in the warm weather months.

Of course, that casual attitude toward suitable accommodations might have changed by the time the first snow of the season fell. An interesting fact of Montana settlement is that many people left during the winter months—no doubt headed for some locale where the weather was warmer and less severe, such as Salt Lake City or Denver.

Since Montana began as an extremely remote and relatively unsettled territory, its citizens had to find their own way to deal with the challenges.

This included the dark winter months, as well as the escalating violence and robberies brought into their camps and fledgling settlements.

Like other gold discoveries in the West, the discovery of new strikes spread quickly by word of mouth and in the newspapers. The Civil War commenced in 1861, and life in remote Montana partially divided along sympathy lines. The camp at Bannack was further divided by social distinctions between the boom-or-bust miners and the more affluent merchants and businessmen. Accounts of the time recall a lawless and violent place, despite responsible and upright citizens.

That said, the riotous aspects of frontier existence is what stirred the blood and captured diary space. Daily life proved an actual grind in the camp, for both women and men. After working at backbreaking, stooping labor for hours on end in cold mountain run-off water, a man's enthusiasm might dim if gold didn't shine. Performing repetitive, mind-numbing tasks only to find nothing but mud and rocks at the bottom of the pan or sluice rocker made the miners turn to entertainment to break the monotony understandable. While the few "honest" women worked to set up households and to maintain a decent standard of living—much of their work amounted to drudgery as well—they probably looked forward to rare episodes of entertainment as much as the men, even if they had fewer options for genteel pastimes.

Dancing provided a surefire cure for boredom in those early days of Bannack.

"With two fiddlers in town, there were regular dances. The men put on their best flannel shirts, soft collars and neckties, and paid $5 apiece in gold dust to take turns dancing with the thirty women in camp."[3]

Based upon that account, it is not clear whether the miners paid an admission fee to dance with the wives and daughters of the camp, or whether the women were of a more professional variety. Assuming the former, community dances were recorded in Bannack with nary a prostitute in attendance. Still, early Montana founding father Granville Stuart recorded, "Many gamblers and desperate characters drifted in, lured by the prospect of acquiring gold dust without digging for it. It became the custom to go armed all the time."[4]

From those two quotes, a clear picture emerges. What happens in a town where there are many more men than women, a freewheeling atmosphere, and men going about armed? Throw whiskey into the mix, and guns will undoubtedly go off. And that's exactly what happened.

I don't know how many deaths have occurred this winter, but that there have not been twice as many is entirely owing to the fact that drunken men do not shoot well. There are times when it is really unsafe to go through the main street, the bullets whiz around so, and no one thinks of punishing a man for shooting another.
— MRS. EMILY MEREDITH ON APRIL 30, 1863[5]

LAW AND DISORDER

Indeed, the early days of Montana were marred by violence and shady dealings.

As common throughout the West, miners sought to protect their claims and often the first established laws came in the form of miners' courts. Patterned on codes developed elsewhere throughout the mining regions, the courts established the size of claims, dealt with water rights, and criminal matters. Interestingly, civil matters were usually decided by jury, but criminal matters were decided by the entire body of miners in the immediate district. Punishment seldom involved incarceration since jails (if existent) were rudimentary, and the matter of feeding a prisoner proved highly unpopular because food was a scarce and costly commodity. Miners' courts dealt a swift and decisive version of law and order: flogging (rare), banishment (common), and hanging, which became more common in Montana over time.

MORE GOLD TO COME—ALDER GULCH AND VIRGINIA CITY

Using early Bannack as a point of departure, gold deposits along Alder Creek were the next major discovery when a group of men panned the riverbed for nothing more ambitious than tobacco money. The prospectors found enough "color" for a few plugs and quite a bit more. Virginia City, Nevada City, and a host of other gold camps sprang up as a result of that fortuitous discovery. The names of the discoverers remain well-known: Bill Fairweather, Henry Edgar, Barney Hughes, Thomas W. Cover, Mike Sweeney, and Harry Rogers.

This band of six Bannack miners decided to head out together to try some new prospecting. Like so much in life—decisions, coincidences, lost chances, and mishaps determine the course of history. On April 9, 1863, the above-named group was one of two separate bands of miners who decided to join forces. One was led by James Stewart (the brother of Granville) and the second group by Bill Fairweather. The initial plan was for the two groups to meet up at a set location along the Rattlesnake River. Bill Fairweather's group had an apparent stroke of bad luck.

They lost their horses.

Because of this delay, they missed the appointed meeting time by three or four days, and although they followed in the tracks of the Stuart party in the hope of catching up, the Fairweather party met further difficulties. Serious difficulties. They were captured on the upper Yellowstone River by a large party of hostile Crow. From this chance encounter between the Crow and the prospectors, an astounding piece of Montana lore was born.

Henry Edgar, in an interview given to the *Anaconda Standard* on September 5, 1899, provided the following account:

In February, 1863 . . . we had got two days travel below the mouth of Clarke's Fork in the neighborhood of Pompey's Pillar, when we were captured by the Indians. There was no fighting. That would have been sure death, they so far outnumbered us. They took us into camp and made medicine over us for three days.

It was jointly through Bill Fairweather and Lewis Simmons that we were saved. I do not understand why it was, but a rattlesnake would never bite Bill. When he saw one he would always take it up and carry it along with him. They never seemed to resent anything he would do with them and he never killed one. As we were going towards the Indian village he picked up a rattlesnake, and just at the outskirts of the village he picked up another. When the Indians saw him come in with a rattlesnake on each arm they were awed. He put the rattlesnakes in his shirt bosom and Simmons told the Indians that he was the great medicine man of the whites.

They took us into the medicine lodge, where a large bush was placed in the center. They marched us around that several times and finally Bill said if they repeated it he would pull up the sacred medicine bush. They marched us around again and Bill pulled up the bush and walloped the medicine man on the head with it. We then were formed three, back-to-back. We had refused all along to give up our guns and revolvers. The old chief drove the other Indians back with a whip. They had a council which lasted from noon till midnight. In the meantime, we were sentenced. If we proceeded, they would kill us. If we turned back and relinquished our horses we would not be harmed.[6]

The men turned around, relinquished their horses, and made their way into the vicinity of what would become known as Alder Gulch.

On May 28, 1863, the men stopped to rest and set up camp. Bill Fairweather stepped into history (beyond his rattlesnake handling abilities) when he decided to pan for gold in hopes of finding enough color to pay for tobacco. His first pan turned up $2.40. The men knew they were on to something big, and did their level best to keep their discovery quiet and known only to themselves. In that aspect, they failed. When the band returned to Bannack for supplies, others in the town noticed the men acting suspiciously. As a result, when the men tried to sneak out of camp to return to their pay dirt, other Bannack prospectors trailed along behind them.

The rush was on in Alder Gulch. Virginia City sprang up as a result.

CIVILIZATION

Tents went up first, followed by clapboard structures. The first strong hint of permanence would be the rare brick or stone structure. The beginnings of settlement in Virginia City were similar to those at Bannack. Founding father Granville Stuart recorded his impressions in a diary that was later published. In that diary he recorded much of the minutia of daily life.

There were no houses to live in and not much in the way of material to construct houses. Every sort of shelter was resorted to, some constructed brush wackiups [sic]; some made dug-outs, some utilized a convenient sheltering rock, and by placing brush and blankets around it constructed a living place; others spread their blankets under a pine tree and had no shelter other than that furnished by the green boughs overhead.[7]

Stuart also recorded prices. If one considers the costs listed in reference to current dollars, the costs are staggering. Basic necessities had to be freighted in, adding to the cost of already expensive prices. Many of the freighters traveled the distance from Salt Lake City to the mining camps.

Flour $28.00 cwt (with a note that it had gone for as high as $40.00)

Fresh beef at 15 cents, 20 cents, or 25 cents per pound according to cut

Beef tallow 30 cents/lb.

Beef sausage (made from scraps), 30 cents/lb.

Bacon 40 cents/lb.

Sugar 60 cents/lb.

Coffee 90 cents/lb.

Table salt 50 cents/lb.

Keg butter $1.50/lb.

Eggs $1.50 per dozen (with the note "very scarce")

Turnips 25 cents/lb.

Potatoes 40 cents/lb.

Candy $1.50/lb.

Raisins 1.00/lb.

Board—ranging from $16 to $18 per week[8]

High prices were only part of the equation of a precarious existence. Fire remained a continual threat. As with so many other western mining camps and towns, Virginia City was not spared. Stuart recounted how men camping at the upper end of Alder Gulch accidently set fire to dry grass. As the wind blew, the fire caught and spread with such rapidity that "many who were camped along the creek and in the brush, had no time to remove their belongings and lost everything they had."[9]

Of course, as was natural for all such improvised settlements, the inhabitants regrouped quickly, and life continued much as it had before.

Lord Dunraven visited the fledgling town and was less than impressed by what he encountered. In *The Great Divide*, he opined, "Good Lord! . . . a street of straggling shanties, a bank, a blacksmith shop, a few dry goods stores, and bar-rooms constitute the main attractions of the 'city' . . . the whole place was a delusion and a snare."[10]

Saloons, whiskey, and Wild West behavior abounded in this newest camp. "Tanglefoot" whiskey was the drink of choice, no doubt with slight variations on the recipe depending upon the ingredients at hand. Stuart reckoned the concoctions consisted of "a quantity of boiled mountain sage, two plug tobacco steeped in water, box cayenne pepper, one gallon water; so if any one got low in whiskey, he manufactured some more."[11]

One of the more amusing accounts of whiskey came from the observations of a miner named Robert Kirkpatrick in 1863.

The whiskey was often made with two barrels of water and a few plugs of tobacco with a quantity of camphor and a little strychnine to give it a tang, to one barrel of pure whiskey; making three barrels of red eye. When the "forty rod" got near the bottom of the barrel it was so dangerous that a man sometimes dropped dead from the effect of a few glasses, having too much "tang" near the bottom of the barrel.[12]

Hurdy-Gurdy House, Virginia, Montana. Men and women dancing in a crowded
dance hall/saloon.
LIBRARY OF CONGRESS. 1867

Indeed, the names for "whiskey" were colorful and descriptive: Tanglefoot, Forty Rod, Coffin Varnish, Taos Lightning, Bottled Courage, and
Dynamite were just a few names that got the point across and drove the
message home.

Dance halls (known as hurdy-gurdies), gambling parlors, and houses
of ill repute abounded—all with the objective of parting a miner from his
money. Conveniently for those on the take, gold dust was the currency of
the time and was valued at $18.00 per ounce. Saloon keepers would take
a pinch of gold dust for a drink. A drink which should have cost $0.25
cents might actually cost $1.00 depending on the size of the gold dust
pinch taken. Men worked in cold, numbing water for hours a day, often
six days per week just to lose their money on game tables or booze . . .
and ladies of ill repute provided companionship. All it took was gold.

CHAPTER 4

HENRY PLUMMER

Prisoner 1573

How many of these persons fell victims to the road agents, on their long and perilous journey, it is impossible to tell; but the inquiries of relatives and friends for hundreds of them for months and even years after their departure, leave no chance for doubt that the villains drove a bloody and prosperous business.[1]

Truth—or an exaggeration?

The details of the vigilantes and their victims are tangled. Much has been written about early Montana's road agents, vigilantes, and the mysterious Henry Plummer. Plummer, through the passage of time, has become the state's most infamous bad guy—but how much is true, and how much is false? What Plummer illustrates is the fine line between the law and the outlaws in the early days, and the possibility of playing on both sides of the equation.

In the haste to deliver swift justice, it remains possible that mistakes could have been made.

The fledgling Idaho Territory (as Montana was then known) provided a home to the phenomenon of road agents, and in response, a group of men known as the Vigilantes rose to prominence. The road agents, acting either solo or in league, preyed upon travelers along Montana's remote roads, helping themselves to gold dust or any other valuables that

Henry Plummer before 1864
WIKIPEDIA. PUBLIC DOMAIN

the travelers carried. According to the chronicler Thomas J. Dimsdale, there were one hundred road agents scattered throughout the territory. He also claimed there were 102 murders committed,[2] although neither statistic has ever been proven. To date, seven named murder victims have been identified, although that number may be higher. Unknown, nameless travelers could easily have fallen prey to the predators and their bodies never discovered.

Ominous warnings advised travelers at the time to proceed with caution, and with good reason. Communication was far more problematic in those days. The telegraph would not reach Montana until 1866,[3] and the mail service proved sporadic based upon a multitude of factors such as weather and availability of carriers. If no one knew a traveler was expected, neither would they have known if the traveler didn't arrive.

Most of the recorded, contemporaneous accounts of those lawless days stand in favor of vigilante justice, but the suspicion lingers that the vigilantism went a few hangings too far. Today that conclusion is all but indisputable, especially taking some of the former vigilantes' interviews into consideration—interviews offered with the benefit of hindsight.

At the birth of the gold camps, many of the miners setting up claims did not know each other. And although the miners were a highly transient population until gold was struck and claims paid off, the merchants offered a modicum of stability. But knowing exactly who to trust proved a very real difficulty with profound consequences if mistaken. All mining camps and towns were built upon a few bedrocks of hard truth. Gold attracted the industrious and the shiftless alike, and all shades in between. The mining camps boasted a freewheeling atmosphere where many conventions of civilization were dropped. Justice was rough, and legal systems were often not yet formally established. Jails hadn't been built, and crime continued. The question of just how to deal with those crimes proved a pressing and serious issue.

According to businessman and vigilante Nathaniel Pitt Langford,

The robbers had their established points of rendezvous on the road, and worked in concert by a system of horseback telegraphy, as unfailing as electricity. Whenever it was known that a person with money was about to leave by coach, a private mark was made upon that vehicle, which would be recognized wherever seen, at Daly's, Baker's, Dempsey's, or Bunton's, the several ranches where the coach horses were changed. Bunton, who kept the Rattlesnake ranche, was the same villain who was associated with Plummer.[4]

Langford supplies vivid accounts of many of the reported robberies. Most narratives are replete with masked men, disguised horses, and shadowy-yet-somehow-familiar figures wrapped in blankets with hoods over their heads. Those "masks" were often flour sacks with the eyes cut out, and anonymity wasn't guaranteed.

Something had to be done about the lawlessness running unchecked. But were the contemporary accounts of that time (written by known vigilantes or vigilante sympathizers) an attempt to partially justify their complicit or implicit activities? Were those accounts offered from fear, or out of an attempt to rationalize events? There seems little doubt that some are an attempt to swing historical judgment in their favor: judgments that might prove inconveniently critical in later years.

ENTER SAN QUENTIN PRISONER 1573

Henry Plummer remains enigmatic, yet he is the most recognizable participant of Montana's early and violent days. Was he guilty, or did he have remarkably bad luck, horrible timing, and a multitude of circumstantial coincidences that only made him appear guilty? Undoubtedly, Plummer fell victim to poor choices of companions, which colored public opinion against him.

Highlighting his movements, the robberies, and the suspicions about him could easily take up an entire book. Over time, the townspeople of Bannack became more and more suspicious of their elected sheriff. A rough outline of the major events provides points to consider:

November 1862—Plummer arrives in Bannack.

January 14, 1863—Plummer kills Cleveland.

May 1863—Plummer is elected as Bannack's sheriff.

June 29, 1863—acting sheriff D. R. Dillingham is gunned down and killed while Plummer was absent for his nuptials.

October 13, 1863—Lloyd Magruder and five men in his party are murdered by road agents. The ringleader is Chris Lowrie.

October 26, 1863—Peabody and Caldwell's stage is robbed between Rattlesnake Ranch and Bannack.

November 13, 1863—teenager Henry Tilden identifies Henry Plummer as one of the road agents.

November 22, 1863—the A. J. Oliver stage is robbed along the route from Virginia City to Bannack. Reported road agents were "Whiskey Bill" Graves and Bob Zachary. This robbery was reported to Sheriff Plummer in his official capacity.

November 1863—Conrad Kohrs traveled from Bannack to Deer Lodge. Kohrs is chased by "Dutch John" Wagner and George Ives with the intent to rob and kill.

December 1863—the body of Nicholas Tbalt (perhaps Tiebalt) is found by an employee of William "Old Man" Clark. He was murdered for the gold he carried to purchase a mule team.

December 1863—a three-wagon train organized by Milton S. Moody travels from Virginia City to Salt Lake City and is intruded upon by "Dutch John" Wagner and Steve Marshland and later attacked crossing the Continental Divide at Rock Creek.

December 8, 1863—Anton Holter on his way to Virginia City to sell oxen survives a murder attempt by George Ives and Aleck Carter, whom he recognized.

December 23, 1863—Bannack's Vigilance Committee is founded.

January 10, 1864—Plummer is hanged in Bannack along with Buck Stinson and Ned Ray.

The details in the above timeline are easily tangled and are still subject to debate about motivations, the adherence to circumstantial evidence, and revenge.

AND SO IT STARTED

In November 1862, Henry Plummer arrived in Bannack with another malefactor, Jack Cleveland, whose real name was John Farnsworth. The two traveling companions arrived after having quarreled over the affections of a woman called Electa Bryan. Without a doubt, Plummer had a complicated past. Once a prospector and sheriff in Nevada City, California, he had also served time in San Quentin for the murder of a man named John Vedder and had been released early due to ill health caused by consumption—now known as tuberculosis. He had also killed a saloonkeeper in Idaho named Patrick Ford, reportedly in self-defense. His traveling companion possessed an even worse reputation. Cleveland, a known "hard man," had broken out of jail in Nevada City while Plummer was a marshal there in 1856. The sheriff at the time, Sheriff Wright, had been killed in the breakout. Considering the strong likelihood that Plummer knew of Cleveland/Farnsworth's past before they set out traveling together, it is remarkable that they kept company. This continued association pointed to the enigmatic character of Henry Plummer. No doubt Plummer was displeased by Cleveland's company, if for no other reason than for the constant reminder of a murky past. Whatever the case, together the two men arrived in Fort Benton, and together they stayed at the Vail's homestead, where both men fell in love with Electa Bryan. Plummer won her affections, proposed, and was accepted. Cleveland's affections were spurned.

Nevertheless, together they made their way down to seek Bannack's gold.

According to contemporary accounts, Cleveland was the more belligerent of the two men. Regarded around Bannack as "a desperado of the vilest character,"[5] and a bully who drank too much, Cleveland often started arguments and was no stranger to hurling accusations. He used his size, vile temper, and readiness to fight to intimidate others. And while the ruffian may not have been out to win a popularity contest, that's exactly what Plummer sought. The hostility between the two men simmered, and then boiled. Openly antagonistic toward Plummer at this point, Cleveland claimed, "Plummer is my meat," meaning that he felt Plummer ripe for the taking. Plummer, for his part, seemed to ignore the taunts and kept his distance as much as possible.

On the morning of January 14, 1863, Cleveland came into Goodrich's Hotel already drunk. Plummer was there, standing with a group of men around the wood stove. Cleveland claimed one of the men named Perkins owed him a debt. Perkins claimed the debt had been paid, and Plummer told Cleveland to sit down. Cleveland sat, but then started making more accusations, including veiled threats about revealing Plummer's past.

"You son of a bitch," Plummer snapped. "I am tired of this."

He drew a pistol and shot first into the ceiling, and then shot Cleveland in the stomach. Cleveland fell to the floor, astonished.

"You won't shoot me when I'm down?," he asked.

"No," replied Plummer. "Get up."

Remarkably, Cleveland struggled to his feet and Plummer shot him twice more—this time in the stomach and in the head.[6]

Cleveland died three hours later.

The murder, by that account, stemmed from temper and happened in broad daylight. Yet many in Bannack believed that Plummer had acted in self-defense, or at least eliminated one of the camp's more notorious bullies. No move was made to arrest Plummer. But other associations from his past would come to haunt him.

Shortly thereafter, a man named Charles Reeves arrived in the gold camp. In another inconvenient coincidence, Reeves was present when Plummer had shot Patrick Ford. He settled in Bannack and "married" a young Bannock woman (from the Bannock tribe). About a week later, the young woman left her marital cabin, fleeing back to her lodge claiming Reeves had abused her. Reeves collected allies and fired into the tent indiscriminately, killing three Bannocks and a French trapper who had investigated after hearing the gunfire.

Fearing trouble, Reeves and his two allies fled town, inviting Plummer to join them. Plummer, worried about retaliation for the shooting of Jack Cleveland, accompanied them. In hindsight, that probably was a bad decision.

The men only made it sixteen miles north of the Rattlesnake Creek when they were confronted by a posse of four men. Plummer, ever the charmer, acted as the negotiator. The men agreed to return to Bannack provided they were given a trial by jury.

Plummer was exonerated, but the men involved with Reeves in the killing of the Bannocks and the French trapper were banished by the first sheriff of Bannack, a butcher named Hank Crawford. Banishment was no small thing, especially in the winter. As customary at that time, the possessions of those banished could be disposed of at public auction to cover costs. Crawford took all the guns left behind and sold them.

The problem came when the banished men were allowed back into Bannack. First Mitchell was allowed back into town, after wandering nearby, cold and hungry. Reeves and Moore had been sent to Deer Lodge one hundred miles north—but after townsmen saw Mitchell in the camp, they deemed it unfair that the other two remained banished, so they were allowed to return as well.

The men were also allowed to have their guns back, causing Crawford to re-collect them and return the money paid—a reversal that undercut the sheriff's authority in no small amount.

At this point, for an undisclosed reason, Crawford started worrying that Plummer entertained designs to kill him. Whether true or not, those hard feelings boiled over into yet another feud.

By early March 1863, the two men—Crawford and Plummer—had started to stalk each other. When tensions boiled over, Crawford stepped out of a restaurant and shot Plummer from behind, hitting him in the elbow. The bullet traveled down his arm and lodged in his wrist. According to legend, Plummer spun around and shouted, "Fire away, you cowardly ruffian"[7] and Crawford did so, but completely missed.

Afterward, Crawford was widely ostracized for shooting a man in the back. He fled to Fort Benton, where he slipped aboard a boat and returned back East.

Plummer's show of nerve, however, served him well.

Despite such a violent, tumultuous start, Plummer was elected sheriff of Bannack in May 1863. Right after that election, he made the decision to leave his new post to marry Electa Bryan. His timing could not have been worse.

The event that precipitated the end of the road agent's hold over the gold-producing districts was the murder of Deputy Sheriff D. R. Dillingham. During the summer of 1863, Plummer left the untried acting Sheriff Dillingham in charge while he left Bannack to marry. To further complicate matters, he appointed several other deputies—men who did not know or necessarily trust each other. The men he appointed were "toughs" by reputation: Ned Ray, Buck Stinson, and Jack Gallagher. In the later part of June 1863, Dillingham suspected some of his fellow deputies were planning robberies and warned several people against them. Dillingham's strongest suspicions fell on Buck Stinson, a barber by trade. But he was also a barber who kept company with a hard-drinking gambler named Haze Lyons. Dillingham warned "Wash" Stapleton of his suspicions, who mentioned the warnings to his companion. In the way of human nature, such rumblings traveled back to Stinson and another blood feud was born.

The trouble spread to Virginia City.

On June 29, 1863, Stinson and Lyons interrupted a mining claim trial in that town and burst into the makeshift courtroom presided over by Dr. Steele. They announced that Dillingham had arrived in town, which obviously meant something to the court recorder named Forbes. Forbes jumped up to join the other two men, and they accosted Dillingham on Wallace Street with pistols drawn and called him a liar. They opened fire, hitting the acting sheriff in the chest and thigh. Dillingham bled to death within minutes.

This attack on a sheriff shocked the Virginia City townspeople. The cold-blooded murder of a lawman in broad daylight and in the main street of town as people looked on bore the hallmarks of something new and defiant.

The three gunmen were arrested and taken into custody by Jack Gallagher, yet another of the deputies appointed by Plummer. The men were restrained in logging chains in a nearby building, guns confiscated. A swift and severe response was demanded by all, causing necessary formalities to be overlooked. Dr. Steele agreed to act as judge, along with two additional physicians, Bissell and Rutar. Gallagher examined Forbes's weapon and proclaimed it unfired.

It must also be noted that Forbes—a clean, good-looking man— found favor in the court of public opinion. So much so that his case was set aside, while those of Stinson and Lyons proceeded. The three judges convicted them, sentencing them to death by hanging. An immediate order for the erection of a scaffold on the edge of town was given.

Next the trial of Forbes took place, and he was acquitted.

The two guilty men were led through town toward the gallows. Lyons broke into tears, and several women in the crowd responded with tears of their own. The sheriff of Alder Gulch stopped the wagon in the middle of Wallace Street and took an impromptu poll asking whether the men should be hanged or not. After several farcical attempts, Deputy Jack Gallagher rode into the middle of the scene and called out, "Let them go! They're cleared!"[8]

Stinson and Lyons fled. Forbes also slipped away from Alder Gulch. Some claimed they recognized him later, going by the name Edward Richardson. Edward Richardson, coincidentally, was the mining partner of Henry Plummer.

TROUBLESOME PAST ENTANGLEMENTS

In light of the multitude of coincidences surrounding Henry Plummer, a look into his past before he arrived in Bannack proves revealing, although the details would not have been known to his Bannack constituents in their entirety.

Plummer had been narrowly elected sheriff in 1856 in Nevada City, California. By contemporary accounts, he conducted himself well. Deemed a rising star, he was reelected in 1857 when just twenty-four years old. The Democrats even nominated him to run for state assembly, but the party split, and he was defeated in the electoral race. All might have still gone well for him in that California gold camp had he not been drawn into a marital dispute between John and Lucy Vedder. Plummer ended up renting his house to the inept gambler and his wife, not knowing the character of either.

The violence between the Vedders escalated to the point that Plummer appointed a police guard for Lucy and even went so far as to send a lawyer to her for council. Deciding she wanted a divorce, Lucy informed her husband of her decision. Vedder blamed that development on Plummer. He threatened to kill both the sheriff and Lucy. On the night she was to leave on the 2:00 a.m. stage, Plummer himself sat guard with her. Vedder came in and fired twice at the sheriff, missing both times. Plummer proved the superior shot.

Lucy ran into the street, screaming that the sheriff had murdered her husband.

Two trials later, the jury concluded that any man who would send a lawyer to advise divorce must be a seducer, and Plummer was found guilty and sentenced to ten years in San Quentin. In ill health during both trials, he was decidedly unwell when he entered the prison system. A petition for his release circulated and was signed by over one hundred county officials. While not exonerated, Plummer was released on the grounds of "imminent dangers of death from Consumption." Remarkably, he returned to Nevada City, California, this time taking up mining. However, for him, old habits died hard.

Performing a citizen's arrest, he captured "Ten Year" Smith, a San Quentin escapee. Later, he tried the same with another San Quentin escapee named "Buckskin Bill" Riley, who resisted arrest, coming at Plummer with a bowie knife, which he slashed across his forehead. Plummer shot him dead, and turned himself in. The police, knowing Plummer's record, suggested that a fair trial might be unlikely and suggested that he leave town immediately.

Plummer drifted up into Washington Territory, joining that gold stampede. Although still inclined to act the part of the lawman, he hung around with disreputable sorts. In September 1862, Plummer found trouble when he and his friends were ejected from a dance hall by Patrick Ford. The saloonkeeper followed them into the stable, firing away with two guns blazing. In the return fire, Plummer killed Ford. While the saloonkeeper's friends tried raising a lynch mob, Plummer escaped east of the Bitterroots—intent at this point on returning to Maine, where he had been raised. Instead, he made it as far as Fort Benton. Awaiting his steamer, a government official rushed into town looking for volunteers to help defend a Sun River farm against an anticipated attack. Both Plummer and Jack Cleveland volunteered assistance. And the rest, as the saying goes, is history.

PLUMMER RETURNS TO BANNACK

Six weeks after Dillingham was shot, Plummer returned to Bannack with his new bride in July 1863.

Plummer, in a bid to extend his authority, rode circuits between Virginia City and Bannack—a two-day ride back and forth between the towns. His efforts made a good impression, and at that time he eschewed former companions and forsook saloons. The finger on his left hand remained permanently crippled from the bullet lodged in his wrist, and he bore the scars of a violent frontier existence. Appearances aside, Plummer during this time tended well to administrative duties. Although still the territorial capital, Bannack lost popularity in favor of the larger strikes in the Alder Gulch area.

Despite Plummer's attention to duty, suspicions started surfacing for Langford. In his accounts, he wrote that he visited a livestock ranch and saw a fine horse that caught his attention. He asked about the horse and was told it belonged to the sheriff, who exercised it but never rode it into town. The suspicions of criminality perhaps had not fully formed at this time; however, that information struck Langford as odd.

Plummer's star still rose in certain circles; he was nominated for the post of deputy marshal and endorsed by the Union League. Many people retained their confidence in him. However, when Langford mentioned his nomination to leading miner Samuel T. Hauser, Hauser warned vehemently against appointing Plummer to be a federal marshal. He argued that if there was a criminal class in the district, Plummer was in league with them, if not their mastermind. Based upon Hauser's warnings, the Union League withdrew their support for Plummer's appointment. Langford recalled when thus informed, Plummer "used many oaths and epithets." From that point on, the two men were at odds and never spoke again. No charges, however, were made against Plummer, and he continued performing his appointed duties.

Then came the murder of Lloyd Magruder and his party in the later part of October. Magruder was another "acquaintance" from Plummer's old California days.

Langford also recounted a tale of traveling with Sam Hauser, who carried $14,000 in gold dust. In a Bannack saloon, Hauser handed the pouch of gold to Plummer for safekeeping in front of many witnesses. The following morning, Plummer returned the pouch along with a gift—a red scarf for Hauser, ostensibly to keep him warm on the journey to Salt Lake City. The red scarf, Hauser felt certain, was intended to mark him as the carrier of the gold for easier identification by the road agents. This tale has gone down in Montana lore, whether or not it is true.

Langford and Hauser made it safely to Salt Lake, with their gold dust intact.

The account of the murder of teenaged Nicholas Tbalt proved far more serious. The youth's body was found by a man out hunting, named Palmer. Palmer approached a nearby "wakiup" to ask for help with the body. There he met Long John Franck and George Hilderman, who refused assistance, saying that people were killed in Virginia City every day, so why should they bother themselves—or words to that effect. Without assistance, Palmer managed to get Tbalt's body into a wagon and drove the corpse to Nevada City. According to Dorothy Johnson, "twenty-five men rode out in a rage," back to the wakiup. There they found Franck and Hilderman with the addition of George Ives and one of Tbalt's mules. The three men were arrested and delivered back to Nevada City. George Ives was tried first on December 19, and his trial reportedly lasted two and a half days. Found guilty after deliberation, he was hanged on December 21, 1863. Long John Franck and George Hilderman were tried and both were found guilty. Hilderman was recommended for mercy and left the region. Franck, who had testified against Ives, went free despite the verdict.[9]

On December 23, 1863, a Committee of Vigilance formed. Things were about to change.

CHAPTER 5

THE NOOSE
TIGHTENS

We the undersigned uniting ourselves in a party for the laudable pur-
pose of arresting thievs [sic] & murderers & recovering stollen [sic]
property do pledge ourselves upon our sacred honor each to all others &
solemnly swear that we will reveal no secrets, violate no laws of right
& never desert each other or our standard of justice so help us God as
witness our hand & seal this 23 of December AD 1863.[1]

Plummer must have viewed the Alder Gulch movements with alarm.
According to accounts, Plummer warned anyone in Bannack who cared
to listen that the Vigilance Committee would hang those who stood in
their way—and that he expected to be a target alongside his deputies Ned
Ray and Buck Stinson.

He wasn't wrong.

John X. Beidler was a member of the vigilantes. He claimed to
have exchanged pleasantries with Plummer's deputies in Bannack but
encountered them again at the Rattlesnake Ranche, where he was "pes-
tered" with questions about the Vigilance Committee. That questioning
left Beidler with the impression they feared the vigilantes would come
for them personally. Stinson, implicated in Dillingham's death, had
cause for worry, and both deputies were suspect for their "odd conduct
in the aftermath of the robbery of Leroy Southmayd."[2] Vigilantes were

indeed on the way, and as soon as Beidler left the Rattlesnake in the morning, he encountered the Williams posse. He directed them to Stinson and Ray—but the posse's sole purpose was to hunt down a man named Red Yeager. The posse stopped at the Rattlesnake Ranche; Stinson opened the door but much to his surprise they didn't want him at all. Stinson directed them toward a small lodge containing Yeager, and quickly left the Rattlesnake as the posse rode away. The Williams posse captured their man, charging him with warning another fugitive named Aleck Clarke. For this, Red Yeager was hanged, but not before divulging names. Prior to his hanging, the leader of the posse asked for a vote as to whether Yeager and George Brown (who testified in the defense of George Ives) should be hanged on the spot. To vote, they should either step to the right or to the left. One man dissented. And the other men leveled their weapons at him. At this point, Williams started having misgivings. Nevertheless, both Yeager and Brown were hanged. The signs on their corpses proclaimed: "Red! Road Agent and Messenger" and "Brown! Corresponding Secretary." According to lore, their bodies were left dangling from the tree for several days. This double hanging took place on January 4, 1864.

On January 10, 1864, Sheriff Henry Plummer and his two deputies Stinson and Ray were rounded up by the Bannack Vigilantes, tried in secret, and hanged.

The killings would go on.

In Virginia City to this day, graves of five road agents have become a tourist destination, or at least a photo opportunity. They lay in a row, surrounded by scrub and by sagebrush—the gently sloping countryside stretches out wide around them. The men's names are painted on wooden boards overlooking the town in the distance. On Wednesday, January 13, 1863, Paris Pfouts and his executive committee held a private meeting in Virginia City. The outcome determined that Jack Gallagher and Hayes Lyons would hang for the murder of D. H. Dillingham. Frank Parish of the Rattlesnake Ranche would hang for his supposed participation in stagecoach robberies—his name being divulged by Yeager before he was hanged. Another man called "Clubfoot George" Lane was also sentenced. He worked in Stuart and Dance's store as a cobbler. The vigilantes

Boot Hill, Jackson Street, north of Cover Street, Virginia City, Madison County, Montana.

believed that Lane had acted as Plummer's spy because he had ridden to inform the sheriff of George Ives's arrest. Previously, Lane had been accused of stealing horses in the Washington Territory, and while those charges were used against him as part of the justification for hanging—those charges were never substantiated.[3] The fifth man was Boone Helm, condemned out of general principle.

As would be Jack Slade a few days later.

The five were arrested at gunpoint; scores of men had been posted around Virginia City on January 14, 1864, armed and ready. According to miner John Grannis, he and the other men were "obeying a notice of the vigilance committee."[4] The men were rounded up and brought into a store on Wallace Street to plead their cases. All men protested their innocence initially. After interrogation, Parish admitted to the holdup of a stagecoach carrying "Bummer Dan" McFadden, and Lyons admitted his involvement in Dillingham's murder. Gallagher and Lane denied any wrongdoings. Apparently, the committee had hoped that the men would implicate the already deceased Plummer, but this they did not do. Nevertheless, the men were marched out of the store, into the street, and over to Clayton & Hale's unfinished drug store. Five ropes had been thrown over a beam. The men asked for a prayer or a chance to write a letter—with the exception of Helm, who asked for whiskey. The men were lined up and lifted onto the barrels underneath each rope. Lane jumped off his barrel before ordered to do so. He fell nearly to the ground, struggling and strangling. Helm reportedly called out, "Every man for his principles! Hurrah for Jeff Davis!" He jumped, and his neck snapped. For two hours, the five corpses hung next to each other, providing a gruesome spectacle.

To continue with that gruesome vein, in 1907 Clubfoot George's grave was disturbed—dug up in fact. His club foot was removed from the rest of his skeleton. The artifact was displayed in a local museum until 2017, when the actual bones were cremated per his descendant's request. A replica of the foot remains as a grim token of a dark time.

A man named "Aleck" Davis proposed that from then on, after the five hangings, anyone accused of a crime should have the benefit of a people's court in the presence of lawyers, juries, and public witnesses.

The secret trials held in Bannack and Virginia City, according to Davis, must not be repeated. He made his appeal to Pfouts and the executive committee—and was made a judge.

This did not mean that the vigilantes' activities ceased, but merely that it seems they knew their days were numbered.

Granville Stuart, a man who chronicled events of the day, noted in his diary of February 24, 1864, "Slade and Fairweather on a drunk today." Fairweather was the rattlesnake charming prospector who discovered gold on Alder Gulch. J. A. Slade was recent of Colorado, but he followed his fortunes to the Montana Territory.

He would come to regret that decision.

Joseph Alfred Slade was born in Carlyle, Illinois, on January 22, 1831—the son of an Illinois politician, Charles Slade, and Mary Dark Kain Slade. Jack served in the Mexican War during 1847–1848 in Santa Fe, New Mexico. There is plenty of lore about Slade, often called "Black Jack,"[5] who harbored a mixed reputation. His reputation, at the time, was so well-known that none other than Mark Twain wrote about him. He claimed that Slade "was the cruelest looking man" he had ever met.

Slade's reputation started in Julesburg, Colorado, where he was hired by Russell, Majors & Waddell, more commonly referred to as the Pony Express.

An unscrupulous stationmaster named Jules Beni ran the stage stop on the Colorado plains, and there were robberies suspiciously close to the station, reportedly by men "dressed up" as local tribesmen. There were also accounts of horse thieves in the area. Slade, upon hearing of the shenanigans, headed out to resolve the issue once and for all. He fired Beni. He reportedly then found company horses being used by the former stationmaster, returning them to the stables over Beni's objections.

In retaliation, Beni and his gang ambushed Slade, shooting him repeatedly and leaving him for dead.

Miraculously, Slade did not die. He did, however, have a vendetta against Beni. He tracked the man and killed him in the Wyoming Territory. The story goes that he nailed one of Beni's ears to a corral or fence post, and the other he reputedly wore as a grisly souvenir.

Slade returned to employment with the Pony Express. At some point he married a woman named Virginia and named the Virginia Dale stage stop after her.

In 1863, Virginia and Black Jack moved up to Virginia City, Montana. The story goes that Slade had been fired on account of one drunken spree too many.

On the one hand, he was smart and a good worker. When he was sober. On the other hand, he had a violent temper when drunk. The problem, according to contemporary sources, was that he was often drunk. Even noticeably so, on the hard-drinking western frontier. Nevertheless, the couple made their way north, where once again the duality of Jack's nature came to haunt him. He had one spree too many, and the vigilantes arrested him as a menace to decency, or something along those lines. On March 10, 1864, he was given time to write to his wife before his hanging. A fast horseman raced to where they lived, and Virginia galloped down to where the hanging was to take place.

She arrived only moments too late.

When Jack Slade's body was cut down, the bereaved widow cursed the town and swore that he would never be buried in that territory. Virginia decided to take him home to Illinois for burial. A special coffin was made, and his body, so the story goes, was preserved in whiskey. Virginia started the journey home with Slade's coffin, but by the time they reached Salt Lake City, the body began to stink.

Slade's body was transferred to the Salt Lake City Cemetery and buried in the Stranger's Lot, Grave Location Plot–B, Block–4, Lot–Pauper, Grave–116, "to be removed to Illinois in the fall." But no one ever came for the body of Jack Slade.[6]

Whiskey proved his undoing all the way around.

To all whom it may concern:

Whereas divers [sic] foul crimes and outrages against persons and property of the citizens of Montana have lately been committed and whereas the power of the civil authorities, though exerted to its full extent, is frequently insufficient to prevent their commission and to punish the perpetrators thereof, now this is to warn and notify all whom it may concern that the vigilance committee, composed of the citizens of the territory, have determined to take these matters into their own hands and to inflict summary punishment upon any and all malefactors in every case where the civil authorities are unable to enforce the proper penalty under law. The practice of drawing deadly weapons, except as a last resort for the defense of life, being dangerous to society and in numerous instances leading to affrays and bloodshed, notice is hereby given that the same is prohibited and offenders against this regulation will be summarily dealt with. In all cases the committee will respect and sustain the action of the civil authorities. This notice will not be repeated and will remain in full force and effect from this day.

SEPTEMBER 19, 1865, VIGILANCE COMMITTEE [7]

Interestingly enough, the notice was posted on page three of a four-page edition. At this point in time, there is no mention or reference made to the mysterious Vigilante code 3-7-77.

CHAPTER 6

CLASH OF CULTURES: 1860S

THE MORE EMIGRANTS AND SETTLERS TRIED THEIR LUCK IN MONTANA, largely on account of the gold strikes, the more disputes arose with the various Native American tribes already in residence. Battles were fought, alliances forged and broken, families shattered, wars waged, people taken hostage, and massacres carried out. All in the name of expansion. Western US history is rife with broken treaties, broken promises, and deaths. Deaths resulted on both sides, although statistically the various tribes fared far worse than the gold seekers and settlers by the numbers.

Trust proved hard to come by, and no one had it easy.

Conflicting priorities, claims, desires, and everything that came with them collided in this decade and would have profound implications on the next twenty years to come.

So much of the struggle came down to individuals and personalities.

Unlike the fur trappers and traders who often married into the local tribes and raised their children as a blend of the two cultures, most of the new settlers did not intermarry. Some notable exceptions took place, such as one of Montana's most illustrious early settlers, Granville Stewart. At the age of twenty-seven, he married a Shoshone girl named Awbonnie Tookanka on April 15, 1862. Estimates for her age vary from twelve to fifteen, but she bore him eleven children, and the marriage lasted until her death at age forty-one from puerperal fever. Several of Montana's founding fathers also married women from the various tribes, including

James Stuart (Granville's brother) who married a Bannock woman in 1863. Her name has been lost over time, and for undisclosed reasons that marriage didn't last out the year. Stuart's second wife was named Ellen Lavatta and was of mixed Shoshone and Mexican blood. That union proved longer lasting—seven years.

But marriages are always a personal matter, and an individual union's success or failure cannot be guaranteed. While some of the bicultural marriages worked well and the participants helped bridge cultural divides, most people in Montana's settlement years firmly identified with one camp or the other—tribal or white. Troubles arose with frequency. Captives were taken and innocent people killed as men fought on both sides for control of the land. Beginning in the 1860s, room for compromise dwindled.

And while gold mining continued, the subsequent years turned out to be rough and bloody hundreds of miles away on the Montana plains.

In 1863, the Bozeman Trail was established as a cut-off from the Oregon Trail to reach the gold quicker. Angling through Wyoming outside of Glenrock, the new artery turned north through the Powder River Basin destined for Virginia City. This time-saving route was conceived of and laid out by failed gold-seeker John Bozeman of Georgia and "old mountain man" John Jacobs, as contemporaries described him. The two men blazed a geographically sensible trail that skirted the eastern flank of the Bighorn Mountains and then veered westward toward the Yellowstone region. The route would prove successful but ultimately hard to defend. An emigrant's usage of that trail came down to a choice and a gamble: of whether time savings or safety held greater value for those making the journey.

The problem with the new route right from the start was not one of geography or the terrain it crossed. The problem with the trail was the fundamental, and deadly, fact that the route blazed right through the prime bison hunting grounds of the Lakota, Northern Cheyenne, and Arapahoe—not to mention the Crow who were guaranteed that land by treaty. The Crow, however, had been pushed west by the Sioux, causing another friction in the region. The native tribes had rights to the land guaranteed under the Fort Laramie Treaty of 1851, not that the emigrants took such legalities seriously. That newly blazed route split

The winter camp. Two Apsaroke on horseback outside a tipi in a snow-covered thicket.
LIBRARY OF CONGRESS. EDWARD S. CURTIS, PHOTOGRAPHER

and scattered the bison herds. To protect their valuable hunting grounds, the tribes would ably and aggressively defend that region without mercy. During Bozeman and Jacob's first attempt to pioneer their new cut-off, the two men soon discovered they were being followed by Sioux, who overtook them on the Powder River. The warriors confronted Bozeman and Jacobs and stole their horses, ammunition, and guns—in short, leaving the men to die. However, the Sioux did not outright kill them. Left to take their chances and make their way back to whatever civilization they might reach, the men set out walking—wandering foot sore and starving—eating only grasshoppers along the way. Against enormous odds, both Bozeman and Jacobs survived to reach the Missouri River, where they located assistance.

Most men would have dropped scouting out the route right there and then, but these two intrepid explorers remained steadfast in their quest to establish a quicker route to the Montana gold. The first wagon train gathered to cross what would become known as the Bozeman Trail.

46 wagons with 89 men, 10 women and several children left Deer Creek on July 6, 1863. Bozeman led the group, accompanied by Jacobs and another guide, Rafael Gallegos. They had traveled just 150 miles when they were confronted by a large party of Northern Cheyenne and Sioux warriors, who warned them to turn back or be killed.[1]

The wagons turned back. Some intrepid explorers pressed forward. Together with nine men, the party including Bozeman continued onward, riding through the nights and sleeping during the days to avoid detection by hostile tribes. In twenty-one days' time, the party entered the Gallatin Valley between present-day Livingston and Bozeman. From there, they progressed on to Virginia City, proving the route could be "done"—but done at a cost with considerable risk. Nevertheless, in 1864 Bozeman escorted another large wagon train. Jim Bridger also led a train through on a new route that he had discovered, traversing the west side of the Big Horn Mountains and down Clark's Fork. Bridger's was a safer yet more circuitous route. Bozeman and Bridger arrived at Virginia City within hours of each other.[2]

In July 1864, an emigrant train of one hundred and fifty wagons reached the gold fields over the Bozeman Trail. According to Grace Raymond Hebard and E. A. Brininstool, coauthors of *The Bozeman Trail*, the "invasion of even one caravan of this magnitude enraged the Indians to hostile activity, for the penetration of this, their land, meant the destruction of wild game and the influx and control by the whites. If fight it must be, the country of the Powder River and its minor streams was an inviting battlefield."[3]

The skirmishes along the Powder River Basin and surrounding areas aside, another dynamic field entered into the mix. On November 29, 1864, the Sand Creek massacre transpired in the Colorado Territory and the conflagration burned throughout the United States's western plains, regardless of boundary, geographic border, or name. The Sand Creek massacre consisted of the savage slaughter of Black Kettle's band of peaceful Cheyenne. Under the protection guarantee of the Colorado

Apsaroke war group. Three Crow Indians—Uphaw, Which Way, and Packs the Hat—on horseback.
LIBRARY OF CONGRESS. EDWARD S. CURTIS, PHOTOGRAPHER

government, elements of the Colorado First Volunteer Infantry and the Colorado Third Cavalry (known as the Bloodless Third) arrived on the scene. More of a militia than a proper military unit, the Bloodless Third was composed of "100-daysers," meaning volunteers who signed on for a hundred days to fight, and their nickname came from their lack of battle experience.

They would have their experience, and their hands would be bloody before long.

The early dawn hours of that fateful day were shattered by cannon and gunfire as the horrific assault took place. As a result, tensions flared at the flagrant disregard for treaty and the code of civilized warfare. Word of the atrocity spread, and warriors throughout the plains exacted revenge.

Although the Colorado massacre was hundreds of miles away, its impact was felt throughout the entire American West. The raiding and subsequent fall of Julesburg, Colorado, *twice* unsettled the region. Although retaliation began along the Platte Road in the Colorado/Wyoming/Nebraska region, the backlash soon traveled further north. White settlers felt a strong need for a military presence in the West. Montana proved no different as it begged officials for protection.

Enter two more men to be reckoned with: Brigadier General Thomas Francis Meagher and General William Tecumseh Sherman. To say that those two men did not get along is the understatement of their century.

The American Civil War raged from April 12, 1861, to April 9, 1865, but that didn't mean that mining ceased, that gold wasn't discovered, and that fortunes were not to be made—because they were. Those fortunes and discoveries were only accessible in practicality by crossing through Native land. Often the mining and extracting took place on treaty land as well. In other words, the whites trespassed. Not that it slowed anyone down . . . much. The problem from a military perspective remained that the "true" war raged back in the east and the south—not in the disturbances of the American West. However, gold funded armies, and settled territory played a critical part in the American expansion. All of which required a measure of protection and support.

And there simply weren't enough men to go around.

The US government's coffers were draining.

By spring of 1865, the Bozeman Trail shut down to emigrant traffic, although the military still used the route. The heaviest bloodshed along the Bozeman Trail was sparked by Brigadier General Patrick Connor, who attacked an Arapahoe Village of five hundred (the Connor Battle of 1865) on August 29, 1865, near present-day Ranchester, Wyoming.

In 1866 the trail reopened to civilian traffic, but instead of merely gold seekers this time around, the people using the trail were those bringing the trappings of civilization—merchants, freighters, and others with goods to sell and equipment to furnish. Trouble with local tribes remained foremost in everyone's minds, and travelers were required to obtain permission to cross on the Bozeman Trail.

Back to Meagher and Sherman.

In 1865, a well-known Irish orator and Civil War veteran stepped from a stagecoach in Bannack on September 5th. Appointed as secretary of the Montana Territory by President Andrew Jackson, Meagher arrived never having previously stepped into Indigenous country. Meagher's life began in Ireland, where he was educated by the Jesuits. In 1847 he was sentenced to death by hanging for treason against British rule. That sentence was commuted to exile in Van Diemen's land, now known as Tasmania. He escaped from there in 1852 and made his way to New York, leaving a heavily pregnant wife behind. The unfortunate woman died shortly after giving birth, and tragedy was compounded when Meagher's son died four months later.

In New York, the Irishman made a name for himself as a nationally recognized orator, newspaper publisher, attorney, Central America explorer, and the leader of the Irish Brigade in the Civil War, where he fought at Antietam and Fredericksburg and rose to the rank of brigadier general. His career in the Union Army succeeded notably; however, his service was marred by frequent accusations of intoxication.[4]

Such accusations didn't slow him down.

Meagher traveled from St. Paul to Bannack, having requested and been denied a military escort, leaving him to proceed along the safer, southern route into Bannack. While in St. Paul he learned of the "risk to white settlement," and upon arriving in the Montana Territory, he wrote to Brevet General Frank Wheaton, commander of the Military District of Nebraska: "The circumstances of this territory require the permanent presence, within it, of a very efficient military force."[5] Meagher's request, forwarded to Brigadier General R. E. Conner attached to the Division of the Missouri Headquarters in Omaha, was declined at that point in time. Meagher's duties continued regardless, and one of his first assignments in the territory was to attend a treaty council in Fort Benton. Upon arrival on November 16, 1865, Meagher's party met a vast number of Blackfoot Nation, reportedly in the thousands. While that may have been an exaggeration, the Blackfeet wore their finest clothing complete with painted faces. The Gros Ventres, Blood Piegan, and Blackfeet arrived for the negotiations—all being considered as members of the same nation. The treaty's intent was to ensure peace between the tribes and, more important, with the US government. To accomplish this goal, the negotiations ceded all the land south of the Missouri River, from the Teton to where it joined the Marias, and again south of the Marias to where it joined the Missouri. The land extending north of these river boundaries would be established as reservations where whites could not settle but *could* build roads.

Meagher signed the unnamed treaty as both acting governor and acting superintendent of Indian Affairs. Over forty tribal leaders made their mark. He left afterward, but trouble broke out immediately. Meagher returned to Fort Benton after commandeering a small cannon from a wagon train of emigrants. He threatened the belligerents that he would fire that cannon unless the four hundred warriors dispersed before nightfall, which they did.

Although Meagher presided over the treaty, he had his own opinions about the proceedings. He told a Democratic Convention held in Virginia City that he had only signed the treaty to dignify it, and that he disagreed with the government's standard practice of bribing Native Americans with token payments, food, and trinkets to induce them to sign documents the government never intended to honor.

In short, Meagher accused the US government of acting in bad faith.

The treaty was never ratified due to a complicated chain of events, but this lack of ratification would cause problems for both Meagher and the Piegan tribe.[6] The Blackfeet didn't have a specified reservation because of the lack of ratification. In practical terms, when determinations between hostile and peaceful tribal bands were sought, it was typical to call the groups back to their reservations. Those who stayed away were deemed hostile. Since the Blackfeet had no recognized reservation to return to, thus signaling compliance, they were assumed hostile by default.

RED CLOUD'S WAR: 1866–1868

Although the 1865 treaty called for restraint of violence between the tribes, that was not what happened. There was hardly even a lull in the action. Hiram D. Upham, a clerk left in charge of the Blackfeet agency on account of his superior, Gad Upson, having tuberculosis, wrote to Upson on February 2, 1866, stating that the Natives were killing whites and stealing horses, and sometimes stealing from each other. Equally disturbing was the return to the vigilante justice that had blossomed only a short time earlier in Virginia City and Bannack. Men in Fort Benton took up arms to quell the violence, as evidenced in a letter written January 10, 1866, and published in the February 3, 1866, edition of the *Montana Post*, illustrating yet another instance of vigilantism in Montana's history.[7] Meagher again asked for military assistance. On February 17, 1866, Sherman, via the Department of Interior, received Meagher's request that regular army cavalry troops be sent out to Montana—a commodity of which Sherman had precious little.

It was an open secret that Sherman and Meagher disliked each other. Yet Sherman tried to explain that he had only "one regiment of Regular Cavalry, the 2nd, for all of Montana, Dakotah [*sic*], Nebraska, Colorado, Kansas and New Mexico."[8] History would bear out that any military effort in Montana that involved both Meagher and Sherman was doomed to failure.[9]

Sherman provided a measure of hope in that assistance might be provided along the emigration routes to Montana. It might have been a token assistance in some cases, but something was better than nothing. The stark fact remained that once the emigrants arrived in the territory, for the time being, they would have to fend for themselves.

As was characteristic of Meagher, he refused to take no for an answer. On April 20, 1866, Meagher wrote to the Indian Affairs commissioner complaining about the lack of military presence, which might have had an effect. In the spring of 1866, eight companies of the Thirteenth Infantry proceeded to Montana under the command of Major William Clinton. Surprisingly enough, those troops weren't stationed anywhere near the gold fields or the Bozeman Trail. Instead, they were placed in a remote location approximately one hundred miles downstream from Fort Benton, sitting at the confluence of the Missouri and Judith rivers. The installation was to be called Camp Cooke, and the location had been scouted out the previous summer by Colonel Delos Sackett and General William Tecumseh Sherman.

The outpost never did the slightest amount of good as far as providing safety was concerned. However, it could be claimed that the remote location with its 680 officers and enlisted men protected the Missouri River traffic, which was not inconsiderable. The cargos were rich and often included Montana gold. A total of 680 men to protect a river, when other parts of the state were boiling over and poised to erupt, seemed, then as now, like overkill.

However, help was coming to the eastern section of the territory. In 1866, to protect the Bozeman Trail, three military installations were built along the "new road" as it was alternately called. Fort Reno and Fort Phil Kearney were established in Wyoming, and Fort C. F. Smith was built in Montana—each with the specific goal of keeping the road open and the travelers safe. These forts provided a small measure of protection for the white settlers coming to Montana. As usual, this same road and the forts built upon it came at the detriment of the tribes and tribal land. The Bozeman Trail ran 545 miles, and the army could only staff some thousand men to patrol the area and hold down the forts.

It wasn't enough.

On November 2, 1866, the telegraph arrived in Montana, thus establishing stronger contact with the States. Of course, those telegraph lines never reached remote Camp Cooke, once again diminishing its value to the territory and causing many to question the outpost's purpose.

This year of advancing settlement and attempted subjugation of the tribes did not go as well as the government hoped. The inhabitants native to the land were not prepared to go without a fight, and able fighters they were.

In December 1866, the Fetterman massacre took place in Wyoming, an event which further set frontier nerves on edge. Ninety men under the command of Captain William J. Fetterman were killed along the Bozeman Trail.

There were no survivors.

"Give Me Eighty Men and I'll Ride Through the Sioux Nation"[10] Such was the reported bravado of Captain William J. Fetterman in November of 1866, a claim that might have sounded hollow at the time provided he actually said it, but the notion of which certainly rang hollow after his slaughter in December of that same year.

As stated earlier, the staffing at the remote forts across the West proved difficult, if not downright impossible. Army strength fell from 1,000,000 in 1865 at the end of the Civil War to 57,000 only two years later. Specifically for the Bozeman Trail, the army was entrusted with keeping peace, providing an adequate measure of safety for emigrants, tending to the east–west telegraph lines, and providing protection for 1,100 miles of the incomplete Union Pacific Railroad and the construction parties building the tracks.[11]

Sioux, Cheyenne, and Arapahoe peoples opposed these developments, the most heartily objected to being the construction of the three forts along the trail.

The army recruits likely were not overjoyed at their assignments either. Due to the remote distances, the nature of their tasks and work detail could prove boring and tedious to remarkably dangerous in turns. For those young men who sought adventure and excitement on the western frontier, the days passed slowly. However, as the days of Red Cloud's War wound down, two important military actions took place. One was Fetterman's massacre in Wyoming, and the other was the Hayfield fight in Montana. Both took place along the "bloody" Bozeman Trail as part of the ongoing skirmishes and clashes.

Noncombatant Colonel Henry P. Carrington was placed in charge of constructing the three forts that were determined as necessary along the

Bozeman Trail. He would become the commander of one of those—Fort Phil Kearney. Fort Reno (later known as Fort Connor) was established in Wyoming, and Fort C. F. Smith (first named Fort Ransom, but later changed) was built in Montana. Another fort was proposed along the Yellowstone, but that idea was abandoned due to lack of available troops.

It was out of Fort Phil Kearney that the tragedy of Fetterman's massacre unfolded. Controversial to this day, Carrington was (and is) viewed as an inexperienced but cautious leader, skilled at organization but having no previous experience with Native Americans. Captain William J. Fetterman, a combat veteran of the Civil War, also had no experience fighting the type of running skirmishes the northern plains tribes preferred. The detail of the day was wood-cutting, known as a wood-cutting train, on December 21, 1866. The woodcutters came under attack, and Carrington sent out Fetterman to lend assistance with the specific order not to cross the Lodge Trail Ridge, which would take him and his men out of sight of the fort. There is no proof that such an order was given, or if it was given, it was simply not followed. Lured by a few Sioux decoys including Crazy Horse, Fetterman fell for the bait and pursued Captain Tenodore. Ten Eyck would later testify that not less than 1,500 and perhaps upward of 2,000 warriors were involved. The common belief is that before the battle started, the warriors were hidden and sprang from the coulees and their hiding places on the far side of the Lodge Trail Ridge, overwhelming the Fetterman detachment of seventy-eight cavalry and two civilians. All in Fetterman's command and the wood-cutting detail were killed. There was not one survivor.

Carrington, upon losing sight of Fetterman, sent out Ten Eyck and a detail of fifty men to lend assistance. He traveled along the road instead of over rough terrain. He was joined about forty-five minutes later by forty men from the quartermaster's department who brought an ambulance and three wagons. These men were later referred to as Citizen Employees.[12]

The hideous task of retrieving the dead soldiers fell to Ten Eyck's command. In his testimony given on July 5, 1867, Fort Phil Kearney, Dakotah Territory, he recounted:

I cannot state the exact number lying at that point as I did not count them, but I think more than sixty. In their appearance they were all stripped stark naked, scalped, shot full of arrows and horribly mutilated otherwise, some with their skulls mashed in, throats cut of others, thighs ripped open, apparently with knives. Some with their ears cut off, some with their bowels hanging out, from being cut through the abdomen, and a few with their bodies charred from burning, and some with their noses cut off. I was able to recognize several whom I was most intimately acquainted with, and among them Captain Brown.[13]

Ten Eyck along with the quartermaster department's wagons and the ambulance were able to bring forty-seven of the bodies back to the fort that same evening. The rest were retrieved the following evening per his testimony.

The reverberations from this disaster would last for decades.

Supplies at all the forts dwindled that fall and winter of 1866 following the Fetterman massacre. Matters at Fort C. F. Smith had become so desperate that only ten rounds of ammunition were available per soldier. On March 25, 1867, John Bozeman wrote a letter to Meagher stating his concerns that settlement would slow, if not cease outright, should the tribes not fall under control. As fate would have it, Bozeman's remarkable luck in escaping serious harm did not hold. In April 1867, he and Tom Cover (pronounced *Coover* and sometimes spelled phonetically) traveled down the Yellowstone, headed toward Fort C. F. Smith. Stopping to make camp, they encountered Natives who stole their horses. The next day on April 18, they were cooking a noon meal and were approached by who they thought were friendly Crow. Instead, they were Piegan and fugitives from their own tribe. Two of them shot Bozeman through the body, as Cover escaped into the bushes.

There is also a Crow version of these specific events.

Apparently, some Crow had been traveling with Mountain Chief and his three sons who were Piegan. The Piegans dropped away, and remarkably the Crow did not notice their absence for a while. When the Crow backtracked, they found that Mountain Chief and his sons had killed

Bozeman. The Crow would end up killing them some years later, according to an account dated April 1, 1896, by George Reed "Crow" Davis.[14]

John Bozeman was thirty-two years old upon his death on April 18, 1867.

Nor did fate deal kindly with Thomas Francis Meagher. He would die a short time later, on July 1, 1867, under mysterious circumstances at Fort Benton. Present at that location to receive a shipment of arms and ammunition for the Montana Militia sent via steamboat by General Sherman, that evening around ten o'clock he fell overboard into the swift current. Supposedly he drowned in the Missouri River. His body was never found.

The summer of 1867 remained tense, and Meagher's death didn't help matters in the territory (although he did have his share of political enemies). Supplies had arrived in early June at Fort C. F. Smith. Along with the better weather, Sioux depredations increased, and the lack of cavalry numbers precluded giving chase.

Although ammunition stores were on hand, fighting strength had dwindled during the spring from desertions and from the departure of parties serving as escorts for emigrant trains. At one point in July, the garrison numbered about sixty effective men, armed with decrepit Springfield muzzle loading rifles. Morale dwindled further when the post surgeon went insane.[15]

On July 17, fortunes turned for the remote outpost. Two companies of the Twenty-seventh Infantry arrived, under the command of Colonel Luther P. Bradley. The Twenty-seventh was accompanied by a small emigrant train and, more important, a Wells Fargo supply train run by civilian contractor A. C. Leighton. The supply train carried badly needed food items and supplies. Of critical value were several crates of .50–70 Allin-modified breech loading Springfield rifles to replace the fort's outmoded, muzzle-loading weapons. The difference in firepower or rounds shot per minute was significant and would prove important. Dependent upon the individual, the muzzle-loaders likely averaged two rounds per minute, while the Allin-modified breech loaders could fire off eight to ten rounds per minute. The tribes were, historically, used to slower shots fired.

The post after Bradley's arrival numbered 350 men strong.[16] Those men created improvements to the existing fortifications, including digging three rifle pits. A strong log barrier was built in the shape of a corral forty feet north of Warrior Creek, which flowed into the nearby Bighorn River from the east. The posts of the corral were screened with willow branch latticework that wouldn't offer much protection when bullets started flying. And they did. The rifle pits were each about ten yards in length, facing away from the river for added defense.

HAYFIELD FIGHT

One of the principal duties at Fort C. F. Smith was to protect civilian hay cutters employed by A. C. Leighton. The hay was crucial for feed for the upcoming winter. The hay cutters chose a location to start their mowing operations about three miles from the fort. The constant threat of harassment or violence from tribes necessitated Bradley sending a daily detachment of soldiers to protect the contractor's men as well as to prevent hostiles from setting fire to the hay, as they had been known to do in the past.

Meanwhile, the Crow, who resented the Sioux and Northern Cheyenne's incursions into their land, warned the soldiers that violence was imminent. The Sioux and the Cheyenne were intent upon continuing Red Cloud's war to rid the Powder River Valley of the forts. Remarkably, the soldiers did not take much heed of the warnings. On July 29, the Crows "admonished the men in the hayfield that an assault upon the post was imminent."[17]

Again, the whites paid little heed.

On July 31, shots were fired at the civilian hay cutters. Lieutenant Sternberg gave chase and drove the Natives off. This was a portent of hostilities to come.

On August 1, the morning followed the usual routine when the civilian hay cutters set to work; a picket took position on a bluff 700 yards away to watch for hostiles and a mounted guard detail stood present while Lieutenant Sternberg and about twenty soldiers whiled away the time that summer morning. About nine o'clock, a shot rang through the valley. Moments later, the picket galloped down from his post to warn that warriors were approaching. Shortly afterward more shots rang out and the hay cutters appeared with their mule-drawn machines, racing ahead.

The Natives reached the rifle pits first before the soldiers could take up their positions. As a result, the soldiers were then forced to take cover behind the low log corral barrier instead. The warriors, believing the soldiers still had the slow muzzle-loaders, charged, and wheeled off. Assuming they had time to attack before the soldiers could reload, they approached again and were repelled by the surprising return of fire. At this point, the warriors started sniping, and some bold individuals crept up and tried to set fire to the branches of the latticework above the fortifications. This attack was successfully repelled, but it cost Sternberg his life when he was shot through the head. He died instantly. For the moment, the warriors withdrew.

The men from the fort used that lull to add to their fortifications. Command was assumed by Sergeant James Horton, but he was severely wounded when the battle recommenced. Now command fell to a civilian, D. A. Colvin. Still, no troops came from the fort as the battle raged on. At noon, the warriors rode off, but they came back later. They even set fire to the grass to try to burn the soldiers out, but the wind shifted direction.

Another soldier, a Lieutenant Palmer, was in charge of a wood gathering detail that morning and saw warriors numbering about eight hundred surround Sternberg's party. The wood cutting detail was commanded to return to the fort, where Palmer reported to Colonel Bradley that Sternberg was badly outnumbered and surrounded by eight hundred to a thousand men. Bradley replied that he did not think it was that many, and that Sternberg could handle them. Later he would write, "I did not know of the fight that had been going on some hours, very little firing was heard, and not a large body of Indians were seen."[18]

Bradley's report was in direct contrast to events as reported by Palmer. Bradley's dereliction of providing relief was later labeled as cowardice by some of the men involved, but the charges were never substantiated and were dropped without disciplinary action.

Bradley, on that day, ordered the troops at the fort into formation with a howitzer at the front. Yet the troops stood, and nothing moved. At around four o'clock, a lone soldier dashed from the battle to the fort, with warriors closing in on him. Finally, the stalemate snapped, and the soldiers opened fire, driving them back. The lone soldier's message was simple, that all would die if help did not arrive soon. That brave soldier's name was Private Charles Bradley of Company E.

Colonel Bradley finally ordered out Lieutenant Shurly with twenty men, who faced fire. More reinforcements were needed, and Captain Burrows rode out to assist. Those reinforcements came under heavy fire as well. Finally, the howitzer was sent out with Lieutenant Fenton and still more soldiers, which drove the warriors back. When the corral was reached, battle debris was strewn about. Two soldiers were killed, with three soldiers and one civilian wounded. Two mules also died.

Due to his inaction, Colonel Bradley understandably lost the confidence of the men serving under him.

The days of the Bozeman Trail were drawing to a close.

The number of emigrants who used the trail range from 2,000 to 3,500 dependent upon the source, but true numbers will never be known. It is believed that thirty to fifty fatalities occurred, although reason of death would likely be the result of disease, sickness, or accident, rather than by skirmishes with the tribes.

By 1869 the Bozeman Trail fell largely unused and was deemed unnecessary due to settlement advances. The advent of the Union Pacific Railroad running through Wyoming opened a safer form of transportation; the settlement on Salt Lake City proved a valuable supply depot; and the sheer expense required to keep the trail open and maintained and the forts manned became viewed as unnecessary and a drain on taxpayer expense.

Thus closed the Bozeman Trail, ending John Bozeman's dream.

CHAPTER 7

CAPTIVES, CAVALRY, AND DESERTIONS

FATES WORSE THAN DEATH

In 1871, a remarkable woman named Fanny Kelly wrote a book titled *Narrative of My Captivity Among the Sioux Indians*. Describing her experiences that led up to the fateful day and the difficulties that befell her in 1864, Mrs. Fanny Kelly recounted the events as they unfolded. This is a rather strange episode in history, both for what happened to Mrs. Kelly and for what happened when she completed her account. Such books about captivity were wildly popular in the day. Upon her release from her ordeal at Fort Sully in South Dakota, she and her husband reunited and moved to Kansas, where he promptly died from cholera. The Larimers, fellow travelers of the same ill-fated wagon train, invited her to stay with them in Wyoming, and that is when the proverbial litigation hit the fan.

> *My leisure hours, since my release from captivity, had been devoted to preparing for publication, in book form, a narrative of my experience and adventures among the Indians, and it was completed. The manuscript was surreptitiously taken, and a garbled, imperfect account of my captivity issued as the experience of my false friend, who . . . escaped after a durance of only one day and night.[1]*

Indeed, upon reading Mrs. Sarah Larimer's account, *The Capture and Escape, or, Life Among the Sioux*, which was first published on January 1,

Jumping Bear Promising by the Moon, to Carry My Letter to the
White Chief at Fort Sully.

Fanny Kelly and Jumping Bear. Jumping Bear promising by the moon, to carry
Fanny Kelly's letter to the White Chief at Fort Sully.
LIBRARY OF CONGRESS. 1871

1870, questions arise. While some of the account is no doubt her own, it
would be next to impossible for a traumatized woman to instantaneously
grasp so much about her captors in the space of less than forty-eight
hours, especially considering the language and cultural barriers.

Leaving Mrs. Larimer's book aside, it is difficult for the modern reader
to accept at face value all of Mrs. Kelly's claims and aggrandizements.

However, there is no doubt she suffered a terrible ordeal. Rape factored in captivity among the northern plains tribes and was far from uncommon, death upon attempted rescue remained a very real possibility, and small children could be put to death if they cried too much or slowed travel. All of which paints a dark picture. To be fair, some captured children were adopted into the tribe and accepted as full-fledged members of a family. Women could be pressed into servitude or marriage, or both. As far as the specter of rape is concerned, Mrs. Kelly claimed no such "personal indignity had fallen to her lot."[2] Of course, that might have been true, but often such a claim was made to avoid blame or disgrace upon eventual return into white society.

The story of Fanny Kelly and Sarah Larimer's capture starts out well enough. On the 12th of July 1864, the small Josiah S. Kelly party headed west. A total of seven persons made up the original band of emigrants: the Kelly family of three—of which one was the Kelly's niece and adopted child, Mary Hurley; two black servants, Franklin and Andy; and their neighbor, twenty-nine-year-old Gardner Wakefield. A Methodist clergyman named Mr. Sharp joined their party, and later they were joined en route by the Larimer family of four, with an eight-year-old boy and a driver for their wagon, Noah Taylor. The Kellys and the Larimers were already acquainted.

The account also makes note of a much larger wagon train traveling at the same time and in the same direction. The Larimer party split off from that larger train to join the Kellys for the benefit of faster traveling time. In due course, the Kelly/Larimer party reached Fort Laramie without incident, where general intelligence reportedly assured the emigrants that hostile tribes were not prevalent.

Near some bluffs in the Wyoming valley of Little Box Elder, according to Fanny Kelly's narrative, 250 war-painted Oglala suddenly descended upon their small wagon train. "Without a sound of preparation or a word of warning, the bluffs before us were covered with a party of about two hundred and fifty Indians, painted and equipped for war, who uttered the wild war-whoop and fired a signal volley of guns or revolvers into the air."[3] At first the Oglala band, led by a chief named Ottawa, professed friendly intentions. The Oglala were fed and given

Josiah Kelly's prize horse as a means of placating them. In an elaborate game of cat and mouse, those friendly intentions turned deadly once the meal concluded.

Three of the combined Kelly party immediately died in the attack, with Gardner Wakefield mortally wounded. Mrs. Kelly's husband, Josiah, had been out gathering wood and, unarmed, hid in the tall grasses and remarkably escaped detection. The servant Andy also survived the attack as did Mr. Larimer—both of whom ran to safety. Mr. Sharp, Noah Taylor, and Franklin were killed outright, and Wakefield Gardner soon died from his wounds. Mrs. Kelley and her daughter, Mary, were taken in the attack as were Mrs. Larimer and her son.

While this was happening, there was apparently a lone wagon tracing along the same route as the Kellys, following behind them at a distance. When it was spotted, some of the Oglala attacked them as well, killing the one member of that party who rode ahead of the wagon.

According to Fanny, the Ogalala proceeded to loot their wagons.

Through all this confusion and turmoil, and completely unknown to the captives, the next day the party's male survivors reached Deer Creek Fort.

Meanwhile, the band of Oglala pressed onward with their four captives and split into separate groups: one containing Fanny Kelly and the other Sarah Larimer.

Now, there are a few strange twists to Mrs. Kelly's story, and one of them begins here. A kind Oglala man named Yechela gave Mrs. Kelly and her daughter some articles previously contained within their wagon—shoes, books, and letters. Fanny dropped papers and letters strategically along their trail without getting caught.[1] Riding double with her daughter, the resourceful Fanny came up with a plan, "Drop gently down, and lie on the ground for a little while, to avoid being seen; then retrace your steps, and may God in mercy go with you. If I can, I will

---

1. Surprisingly, "one of Fanny's notes was found twelve years later by Lieutenant James H. Bradley, 7th Infantry . . . when, on May 21, 1876, he was searching through an Indian burial scaffold near the junction of the Rosebud and Yellowstone Rivers. Among the items buried with the warrior was a paper signed by Fanny Kelly that concluded, 'I am compelled to do their bidding.'" James Bradley, *The March of the Montana Column: A Prelude to the Custer Disaster* (Norman: University of Oklahoma Press, 1961), 113.

follow you,"[4] she told her daughter. Fanny herself tried to escape after a certain distance passed, but her attempt proved unsuccessful. Following the same general instruction she gave her daughter, she quietly slipped down from her horse and hunkered down, low on the ground. "Forming a line of forty or fifty abreast, they [the Oglala] actually covered the ground as they rode past me."[5] Still crouching in the undergrowth, Kelly spooked their horses, which led to her discovery. At her recapture she invented a story, saying the child had fallen asleep, slipped from her arms, and that although she had called to her captors, they failed to hear her. She claimed to have jumped off to search for her child. Although beaten for her attempted escape, her captors promised to send out a search party for the child in the morning's light.

The next day—the second day since the raid—the group traveling with Fanny came across the other band containing Mrs. Larimer and her son. Fanny Kelly admitted her determination to escape to the woman. According to Kelly, "She entreated me not to leave her, but promising help to her should I be fortunate enough to get free."[6]

Because of her attempted escape, Fanny was tied up that night. The next morning when Fanny awoke, she realized that Mrs. Larimer and her son had escaped, despite their conversation the night before. This event is also pivotal in Fanny Kelly's tale of captivity.

Days later as the band was once again on the move, a previously unknown brave rode near Mrs. Kelly. She recognized a brightly colored child's shawl as belonging to her daughter. Worse, she saw a scalp of long, fair hair.

No doubt horrified and mourning her adopted child, Fanny endeavored to survive the ordeal as the band traveled north to the Tongue River and Rosebud Creek. Ottawa, her original captor, traded her to a Hunkpapa Sioux named Brings Plenty. On July 28, Fanny's new village was attacked by Brigadier General Alfred Sully. Two thousand US soldiers fought against three thousand Native warriors. Sully emerged victorious in what would come to be called the Battle of Killdeer Mountain. Afterward, the Hunkpapa fled west. On August 7, 8, and 9, more fights continued along the Little Missouri and the Hunkpapa were pushed toward the Yellowstone with Fanny caught up in the melee.

On September 2, 1864, the band attacked a wagon train of about two hundred emigrants led by Captain James L. Fisk, bound for Montana's interior. These skirmishes characterize a slow simmering, running battle that lasted two weeks.

Purposefully, the Hunkpapa sought contact with Captain Fisk, hoping to get him to lower his guard against further attack. Illiterate in English, the Hunkpapa approached Fanny demanding that she communicate with Fisk on their behalf, asking for supplies. Instead of following instructions as given, Fanny warned Fisk of their intentions. As a result of her communication and learning of her plight, Fisk attempted unsuccessfully to ransom her and offered three horses, flour, coffee, and sugar for her release, but the band wanted forty head of cattle and four wagons.

Terms were not met.

Fisk did, however, make Kelly's plight known to General Sully. On October 23, about two hundred Hunkpapa and Blackfeet Sioux negotiated for peace with Captain John H. Pell, and part of the terms included Fanny's release. This was the point where Sitting Bull reportedly became involved in the proceedings, and Brings Plenty along with a delegation of Blackfeet Sioux delivered Fanny to Fort Sully. Fanny was released on December 9, 1864.

Mrs. Kelly was held captive for five harrowing months of plains warfare. At times, her account varies from official records, often likely inflating her importance in the process. Her husband, during the time of her captivity, reportedly sent many messengers with horses and money for a ransom, but Fanny didn't believe that he had made a serious enough effort for her release. No doubt suffering trauma of his own, Mr. Kelly reportedly found the scalped body of Mary and buried the girl where she fell. Mr. Kelly died of cholera in Kansas in 1867. Shortly thereafter, Fanny gave birth to their son, Josiah Kelly, Jr.

Fanny went on to pen her account, and in April 1870 was awarded $5,000 in damages on account of Mrs. Larimer's suspect version. The court found in favor of Fanny, agreeing that in 1869, Sarah Larimer took Fanny's manuscript to Philadelphia where she had it published under her name only. Fanny sued and received the judgment in her favor. Two appeals followed, and when the dust settled, Fanny's award was reduced to a mere $285.50, with the last hearings dragging out until 1876. On a happier note, she remarried in 1880 to William F. Gordon and worked at the US Patent Office. She also became something of a celebrity on the lecture circuits, where she was billed as "The Queen of the Sioux" and was asked to give her opinions on the current headlines of the time—related to the Meeker massacre in Colorado, with the subsequent captivity of women in that clash.[7]

Fanny Wiggins Kelly Gordon died in moderately prosperous circumstances in Washington, D.C., in December 1904.

THE OTHER WOMAN

Sarah Luse Larimer also received a measure of fame for her ordeal, beyond her lost court battle for plagiarism. According to one newspaper account, Larimer filed for an Indian Depredation settlement and received a "large amount." The newspaper proclaimed: "Soldiers Saved by a Woman—Sarah L. Larimer, while Captive with her Baby, Learned the Plans of the Reds."

The article claimed that Mrs. Larimer had crawled with her baby into the camp of the Eleventh US Cavalry, providing a "detailed account of the movements of the Indians and how plans had been laid to trap the troops, whom they knew were after them." The officers acted upon the information she gave and were successful in their attack on the camp, with the exception of one lieutenant who took a small number of men with him and, disregarding Mrs. Larimer's information, ran into an ambush, where he and his men were killed.[8]

The attack and death of the soldiers may indeed be true, for the Eleventh Cavalry, Kansas Volunteers (First Co.) were involved throughout the West on tribal detail. Through all of their engagements from 1863 through 1865, the "Regiment lost during service 61 Enlisted men killed and mortally wounded and 2 Officers and 110 Enlisted men by disease. Total 173 men."[9]

Fanny Kelly, and to a lesser degree Mrs. Larimer, prevailed over an episode that, while not necessarily a "fate worse than death," came plenty close for Mrs. Kelly. This pervasive fear lurked in the minds of all women chancing the plains: the horror of captivity, rape, or violent death. That fear accompanied all women—emigrants heading West, officers' wives at the forts, and homesteading women.

That fear for officers' wives, which might seem farfetched, came remarkably close to happening at the remote Camp Cooke outpost (also known as Fort Clagett).

At Camp Cooke. May 17, 1868, hostile Indians (Sioux and Crows), numbering about 2500, surrounded and attacked the post at about one o'clock P.M., the attack being continued without intermission until 7 o'clock, when the Indians were driven off, carrying with them their dead and wounded. The garrison at this time consisted of Companies B and H, 13th Infantry, under the command of Major Clinton. The troops during the engagement were commanded by Captain DeCourcy. Fearing that the garrison might fall into the hands of the Indians, the wives of the officers requested that they be placed in the magazine and that the magazine be fired in the event of the capture of the post, in order that they might be saved from falling into the hands of [captors].[10]

One officer's wife recorded the attack in her diary claiming that the women "held a 'council of war'" and determined that if the fort was overrun, "we preferred to be shot by our own officers rather than to be taken captive."[11]

Camp Cooke had been left shorthanded when the attack occurred. One hundred troops had left for summer camp at Camp Reeve on the Musselshell. Only one soldier was killed during the exchange, and that happened by accident.[12] "Shorthandedness" remained a constant theme concerning the forts and outposts during this era.

IN RODE THE CAVALRY

The cavalry patrolled the northern plains as best they could, given the limited manpower and the sheer distances involved.

The western United States was partitioned into divisions. During 1865, the Division of the Missouri encompassed the Territory of Montana. Under the command of William T. Sherman, the massive sector included all states and territories west of the Mississippi River, east of the line of present-day Idaho, Arizona, and Nevada, and north of Texas. The Division of the Missouri covered approximately one million square miles, contained about 190,000 members of various tribes, and was guarded by approximately 18,000 soldiers scattered between seventy-six established forts or posts.[13] On July 28, 1866, the Military Department of the Missouri was reorganized and scaled back, with Montana coming under the Department of Dakota.

That same year, Fort C. F. Smith was constructed along the Bozeman Trail. Several Montana trading posts remained scattered around the territory as remnants from the fur trapping era. Indeed, many of the traders conducted business much as they had since the 1830s—buying up pelts and selling supplies to the frontiersmen and local tribes. Although these posts were called forts, such installations were not the formalized military structures the region desperately needed. Traffic into Montana swelled with the discovery of gold and the accompanying prospectors. After the Civil War, the US Treasury coffers were slender and close to bankruptcy. Although not widely admitted for fear of perceptions, gold provided the impetus for the construction of forts along the Bozeman Trail. Mining drove the Montana economy, although the first census report from 1870 had yet to be delivered. That census enumerated the percentage of Montana males engaged in mining at 49 percent.

When the Civil War broke out, President Lincoln and the Secretary of the Treasury, Salmon Chase, asked the banks in the east for loans totaling $50 million *in gold* to support the war effort. By the war's end, the Union had spent sixty times as much. The government experienced great difficulty raising loans from Europe to fund a war against itself, forcing the Union to turn to domestic sources. Greenbacks were government-based currency, not convertible for gold or silver. The value of the greenbacks steadily declined against gold and caused inflation in the price of goods and supplies. Gold certificates were placed into general circulation in 1865 after the war ended, in order to amass gold coin. The gold certificates proved popular with merchants as they eliminated the need to transport and maintain commerce in heavy bullion, but that same bullion remained desperately needed by the government.

Hence the gold-strapped government's willingness to invest in forts along the gold routes.

C. F. Smith in Montana and Forts Phil Kearny and Reno in present-day Wyoming were established to quell hostilities that might interfere with the commodity they needed so desperately.

After the Civil War ended, the prevailing opinion was that the "Indigenous problem" would be "solved" in short order.

That's not what happened.

As a result, not all forts were well planned nor well established. Fort Laramie in Wyoming provided an example of a well-planned military establishment, while others were little more than outposts clinging to the lonely plains. With anticipated short lifespans, Montana's forts often started out as crude collections of structures. Soldiers' work details included building improvement and maintenance as required, but lumber and supplies proved scarce in many locations. Some of the forts' active lives lasted only two or three years, such as those constructed along the Bozeman Trail.

Life at the remote military outposts could best be described as bleak drudgery—days slipped into weeks, which turned into months, then seasons, and finally years. If a man were predisposed to riding or marching vast distances, the occasional skirmish, and a whole lot of mundane work details, he might have been well suited for the distant posts. Assignment to forts along the Bozeman Trail were a different matter entirely. Duties along that route involved intense fighting and the constant threat of hostilities.

Military order in the western forts, like elsewhere, remained stratified according to rank and privilege, which might have grated against many of the men serving. Enlisted men lived in a communal setting of one large room filled with beds. Sergeants might have had the benefit of small, adjoining private rooms tacked on. Officers "enjoyed" better accommodations, but some might have still been far from ideal. Bachelor officer accommodations were set up in separate structures. Married officers' quarters were often in semi-detached buildings. The post commander might occupy a fine detached house, but then again, it all depended upon the specific location. One of the peculiarities of fort life involved the process of "ranking out"—whereby a superior officer could (and would) take the accommodations of a junior or lower ranking officer. This pattern would continue down the chain until some unfortunate at the bottom of the pecking order ended up back in the barracks.

Whatever the case, after the Civil War, western installations were undermanned and underfortified. Officers were often placed on "detached" duties, leaving the noncommissioned officers (NCOs) in charge of the smaller units. One major sticking point was the low rate of pay. Enlisted men earned seventeen dollars per month, with the NCOs receiving a proportionally higher salary. The unlisted pay rate was *decreased* to thirteen dollars per month in 1871, which obviously eroded moral. All personnel were allotted a prescribed food ration per man each day, which actually was an inducement. For poverty-stricken easterners or newly arrived immigrants, the army provided a reliable means to obtain food, clothing, and shelter. For those struggling to find employment or make ends meet, the army offered an option. This, however, brought in to question the quality of recruits enlisting.

The emotional needs of the enlisted men were likely never considered.

Should recruits be already married, they could bring their wife and family with them, but the living accommodations were spartan. Unmarried enlisted men were encouraged *not* to marry given the difficulties of accommodation, and regulations required them to request permission from their commanding officer to tie the knot. Married officers were able to bring their wives and children to the military outposts. While their living conditions might not have been the most enticing, no doubt they were a far sight better than what the enlisted families endured.

Women, on the rough outposts, proved scare.

Washerwomen occupied a rather peculiar position in fort life. As of 1802, Congress authorized the employment of four laundresses per company, and as such, they were entitled to housing and rations. Their housing was subpar, and they were usually placed in tents or small, drafty dwellings behind stables or warehouses. Commonly referred to as "soapsuds row," these locations were occupied by hardworking women who were deemed as desirable wives by many of the enlisted men on account of their room and board, not to mention the wages they earned.

Washerwomen bore the additional stigma of acting as prostitutes, rightly or wrongly. In all likelihood, there were some prostituting washerwomen, but that depended upon the individual in question. Between the years 1878 and 1883, the army phased out the official laundress position. While laundry remained a task performed by women, it transformed into civilian work.[14]

Hygiene and cleanliness were no simple matter. Of course, the army had regulations. Men were required to wash their hands and faces once a day, and their feet twice a week. A weekly bath was also required in theory, but the availability of water played into its enforcement. Field duty during the stark winter months rendered hygiene regulations near unenforceable. As a result of dirty clothing, hair, and bodies located within close living quarters, body lice known as "gray backs" were an issue. Body lice carried typhus. Disease on the western frontier proved a greater threat than wounds from hostilities.

Inadequate food and supplies also created a pressing concern, especially in the early years. Fort C. F. Smith during the winter of 1867 faced severe food shortages. Freighters delivering food, ammunition, and other necessities were unable to reach the fort due to constant hostilities from the neighboring tribes coupled with severe weather. The troops were reduced to a diet of cornmeal. Should freighters be able to deliver, there were still problems concerning the storage of food and resulting spoilage. Unscrupulous army contractors also contributed to the shortages. Poor preservation, packaging, or improper handling could lead to rancidity or insect infestation. Flour, cornmeal, and rice could harbor weevils if the staples were old. If food was stored in damp conditions, maggots feasted. Unscrupulous contractors often sent the army worthless rations. There are instances of rocks being shipped in food boxes and containers, for which the government paid the contracted price. Men could also develop scurvy from the lack of vitamin C in the early days. As time progressed, posts carried at least vinegar to help ward off that disease.

Diseases and illnesses were prevalent in the western military installations.

The military kept relatively complete medical records. Most injuries and deaths were not caused from battle wounds but rather from the diseases and ailments prevailing in the nineteenth century. While the forts had doctors, hospitals remained understaffed and, should a soldier be wounded in battle, infection often set in. Far more men were lost to malaria, dysentery, diarrhea, cholera, tuberculosis, and venereal diseases than combat injuries. Alcohol, a balm against loneliness and boredom, provided a constant and insidious problem. Medicinally, whiskey was the western cure-all for a multitude of ailments. A readily available tool in the doctor's arsenal, it was prescribed for any variety of infirmities. Alcoholism proved an issue—although hard drinking was widely accepted, and incidents of performance-reducing drunkenness were underreported. Whiskey and beer alleviated the sheer boredom of life in those remote regions, and many, both officers and enlisted men, spent a good portion of their pay on intoxicating liquors. Keeping men sober enough to be fighting fit remained a constant challenge. There are notable instances in important battles, such as the Battle of the Marias, where the officers in question were so drunk that their judgment in battle was seriously impaired.

DESERTERS HAD THEIR REASONS

Considering the remote locations of army outposts far away from civilization, it still may come as a surprise that desertion occurred with regularity. Recruits didn't always know what they were getting themselves into. Some accounts claim that new recruits were delivered to outposts under guard in order to prevent desertion even before reporting to duty.

Men succumbed to desertion due to a variety of factors, but low pay, boredom, lack of decent food, and primitive accommodations all featured. Far from uncommon, desertion tended to occur in the warmer months when a man had a better chance at survival. The Army considered desertion a capital crime, but in the western outposts men were not often executed. Should the deserter be caught, most were incarcerated for a time, then forced to serve out their remaining enlistment. Between the years of 1867 and 1890, an incredible one-third of the enlisted men deserted. A drop in the pay rate for a private from sixteen dollars a month to thirteen a month triggered an increased desertion rate and a decrease in morale in 1871.

An attendant problem of desertion, from the government's perspective, was the loss of army property. Deserters didn't leave their posts emptyhanded but took horses, saddles, food, guns, and whatever else they deemed necessary for their flight. In 1875, the army determined that about two-thirds of its missing handguns were pilfered by those deserting.[15]

Any efforts made to recover deserters varied upon circumstance and the temperament of the commanders in charge. A man with a head start, a fleet mount, and an unknown destination made recovery difficult. Often it was deemed easier to just let the deserted go than to consume further scarce resources that a manhunt would require. Soldiers pressed into pursuit might be the man's acquaintances or friends, also reducing chances of recapture. Even if the deserter was a perfect stranger, a degree of sympathy could be expected from those giving chase.

It almost goes without saying that gold strikes proved a powerful lure for the underpaid and bored enlisted man.

CHAPTER 8

THE BOTTOM OF THE BOTTLE AND THE BOTTOM OF THE BARREL

WHISKEY PLAYED A COMMANDING ROLE IN THE MARIAS TRAGEDY AND in the demise of some of the heavy-drinking men in Montana.

One of the earliest, if not the earliest, account of whiskey or "ardent spirits" made available to the Native Americans is mentioned by Captain Meriwether Lewis. Liquor-induced events in 1806 led to the only bloodshed during the Lewis and Clark expedition. Before the violent events unfolded, Lewis and his party were told of another band of traders they would encounter near the Marias River, conducting an "establishment where they trade on the Suskasawan river." They would "obtain arms[s], ammunition, speritous [*sic*] liquor, blankets &c, in exchange for wolves and beaver skins."[1]

This set up one of the classic models for trade in the Upper Missouri River basin and north into the British possessions. White traders supplied liquor in exchange for pelts.

James Kipp, an early trader originally from New York, was born in 1788. He began his trading career with the North West Company and Kenneth McKenzie—both of which were out of business when the merger with the Hudson Bay Company transpired. Kipp and McKenzie stayed in the region: Kipp working next for the American Fur Company, which later merged with the Columbia Fur Company that McKenzie led. Mergers and renaming of companies occurred with frequency, but the important point of note is that in 1831, Kipp and McKenzie built a post in Blackfeet territory called Fort Piegan.

When the traders went down river the next spring to sell the pelts they had collected, the Piegan burned down their fort.

Somewhat surprisingly, this hostile act did not deter Kipp and McKenzie when they returned to the area. They built a new post, this time called Fort McKenzie, which was a more formal and robust affair than the earlier Fort Piegan. To celebrate the new fort, with an ever-present eye toward commerce, Kipp supplied the Piegan with "200 gallons of specially concocted whiskey as an initial welcome and to encourage them to trade."[2] This resulted in an impressive haul of 6,450 pounds of beaver, from which the company realized $46,000 the next spring. When the popularity of beaver waned, buffalo robes became the main trade: in 1841, over twenty thousand buffalo robes were traded.[3]

But back to the alcohol.

As early as 1832 it became known that the US federal government planned to ban whiskey from tribal territories. In 1834, Congress outlawed alcohol for use in trade. McKenzie was effectively shunned from the fur trade in 1833 due to an illegal still being found and reported. Of course, that shunning may not have amounted to much in his view. He sold the still's product to the tribes for pelts. James Kipp continued to stay in the area, and although he had a wife in Missouri, he married a Mandan woman and fathered a child with her: Joe Kipp, their son, was born in 1849.[4]

Joe Kipp would become directly involved with the Marias massacre.

The Fetterman massacre occurred in December 1866, setting the army's, and the whole frontier's, nerves on edge. On June 20, 1867, Congress appointed a peace delegation to deal with the western plains tribes. Their ultimate motive was to move them all on to reservations. The bill called for a new "scheme," with the plan to establish two large reservations—one north of the state of Nebraska and lying west of the Missouri River, and the other located south of Kansas and west of Arkansas. In the

Senate, the question of frontier protection expense was debated. It was claimed that it cost one million dollars per Indigenous person killed, and one to two million dollars per week to defend the frontier populations.

Considering fiscal concerns, it was deemed preferable to seek peace.[5]

Of course, the government remained very interested in protecting the railroad and securing the overland routes. This was one of those moments in history where the decision was made to attempt to assimilate the tribes via agriculture and reservation life, or to exterminate them altogether.

Meanwhile, trade in Fort Benton carried on using whiskey as one of the primary currencies.

By the autumn of 1867, General William T. Sherman formed a clearer picture of some of the difficulties in protecting and governing Montana. Not only did he want to stabilize the area from the threat of attack by local tribes, but he also wanted to be able to legally, and effectively, police crime involving or committed by whites. Fort Shaw was garrisoned in 1867 in the heart of Blackfeet territory. This fort shifted the attention to issues concerning the Blackfeet, and by extension, whiskey.

George Wright was the "erratic" Blackfeet agent who claimed to be besieged on all sides by Blackfeet and Piegan peoples needing their promised supplies, for food and medical attention.[6] It seems doubtful that the tribes under his oversight received their full allotted and promised supplies. Wright sent a letter to the head of Indian Affairs claiming he had received only one thousand dollars of the amount allocated to the Blackfeet because Governor Green had gambled the rest of the funds away. To make matters worse, while Wright was accusing Green, supplies that had been intended for the Blackfeet made their way into Fort Benton stores to cover Wright's debts. Wright retracted his letter accusing Green, but the writing was on the wall. As his last act as Blackfeet agent, he wrote, "It was during last winter, occupying some five months, that king alcohol continually held high carnival while his admirers were masked in buffalo robes. It was indeed a painful sight to witness the debauchery of the Indians, made so by liquor given them by the whites in exchange for their peltries."[7]

This account confirmed Sherman's suspicions, but Congress failed to approve the army's ability to oversee domestic laws, and the charges went unanswered.

Against this background of corruption, tit-for-tat exchanges, skirmishes, overindulgences of different varieties, and whiskey sales impoverishing Indigenous people, the Marias massacre unfolded. During the summer of 1868, treaties were made with various tribes but remained unratified, meaning no legal reservations were established. Overlooking that very important detail, acting Montana Governor James Tuft announced a treaty on September 28, 1868. The boundaries were exactly the same as the 1865 treaty, which had not been ratified either.

Some of the tribal leaders clearly saw whiskey for the detriment that it was.

Mountain Chief, believed to be the leader of the Piegans, chased away the whiskey traders, claiming if his band wanted to trade, they would go into the forts and leave immediately thereafter. Mountain Chief had previously been publicly accused of killing John Bozeman. Like other leaders, however, Mountain Chief could not always contain the actions of the younger braves.

As all this unfurled, a man named Malcom Clarke, a former trader for the American Fur Company, began to ranch along the Prickly Pear Creek northwest of Helena. Clarke had been married for a number of years to a Pikuni named Cutting-Off-Head Woman, who was a member of Many Chiefs' band, as was her cousin, Owl Child. Many Chiefs' band was led by Mountain Chief. Owl Child had a bad reputation among his band, stemming from a battle where he claimed a kill that most present agreed belonged to another man named Bear Head—a definite affront in their culture. During a resulting argument with Bear Head, Owl Child leveled his rifle and killed him. As a result of those actions, Owl Child became an outcast, although he continued to live with Mountain Chief's band. Described as a bitter man, Owl Child did his best to punish white encroachment by stealing horses and livestock, burning houses, and occasionally killing a miner or settler. In the spring of 1867, several of Cutting-Off-Head Woman's relatives came to visit, and among those visitors was Owl Child, who had the bad fortune of having his horses stolen while at Clarke's ranch. Owl Child blamed Clarke, and in retaliation stole some of his horses, which he drove back to his camp. Malcom Clarke and his son Horace tracked the horses to the camp, where they took them back. Horace struck Owl Child, calling him a dog, and Malcom called him an old woman. These insults, in Pikuni culture, demanded revenge.[8]

On August 17, 1869, Owl Child and twenty-five Pikuni warriors paid a visit to the Clarke ranch on the Prickly Pear Creek. When they left, Malcom lay dead and Horace was grievously wounded. Perhaps no other singular act galvanized Montanans' opinion against the Blackfeet so strongly. To add fuel to the fire, US Marshall William F. Wheeler produced a document that listed fifty-six whites killed and one thousand horses that had been stolen by the Blackfeet in the year of 1869 alone.[9]

The lines were being drawn, and it became increasingly obvious that it wouldn't end well.

Major Eugene Baker, a hardcore, hard-drinking fighter was hand-picked to lead the charge against the Piegan. Additionally, Inspector General James A. Hardie had been called out to Montana to assess both sides of the Blackfeet and settler dispute. Surprisingly, the new agent for

Lt. Col. Baker and officers of Fort Ellis, Montana.
LIBRARY OF CONGRESS. JULY 1871

the Blackfeet, a Lieutenant Pease, claimed that he was unable to provide any information as to the tribe's whereabouts.

Instead of working through official government channels, obtaining information now came down to the traders. The same traders who supplied the Blackfeet with whiskey in exchange for their robes.

The Piegan were known to set up winter camp along the banks of the Marias—according to information supplied by the traders. Decidedly acting in a two-faced fashion, the traders had the chance to warn the tribe of the army's interest and intended strike. As for the interests of the army—they wanted to strike but also wanted to avoid attacking friendly bands.

The tone changed.

On January 15, 1870, General Sheridan issued the command, "If the lives and property of the citizens of Montana can best be protected by striking Mountain Chief's band, I want them struck. Tell Baker to strike them hard."[10]

The day before the orders were issued, Baker rode into Fort Shaw with the four companies of the Second Cavalry. Baker was assigned two additional companies upon his arrival at the fort. Joe Kipp and Joe Cobell—an Italian man who had been married to three Blackfeet wives—found himself in a similar situation to the murdered Clarke. It remains unclear as to the sequencing of his marriages, but his second wife, Mary, was the sister of Mountain Chief. Another similarity was that Cobell had six animals, presumably horses, stolen by Piegan. He also faced threats similar to those issued to the deceased Clarke.

The weather was brutally cold when Baker arrived at Fort Shaw, so much so that the attack upon the camps along the Marias was delayed. However, on January 19, Baker headed out. His force numbered about three hundred and eighty men. At some point in the march toward the Marias, Baker left the wagons and provisions behind. The cavalry, with a few mules laden with provisions, proceeded on ahead. Again, the question of whiskey is raised. One journalist was told by a member of the company that "officers and men, 'tried to keep their spirits up by taking spirits down,' and scarcely knew what they were doing" by the time they reached the end of their journey.[11]

The men traveled by night and lay low during the day. At some point Baker's men broke camp and arrived at the Marias during the dark morning hours of January 23, two days late from their original expected arrival of January 21.

The lead scout of this expedition was Joe Kipp. And Joe Kipp realized that he had made a serious error. He had directed the cavalry toward a camp stricken with smallpox led by Heavy Runner, instead of Mountain Chief's camp. Kipp admitted his mistake and approached Baker. Baker believing that Kipp tried to deceive him for some unknown reason, refused to accept Kipp's attempted correction of his initial mistake. According to guide Horace Clarke, Baker threatened to shoot Kipp.

Again, many (if not all) of the officers and enlisted men's judgment was impaired by the consumption of notable quantities of whiskey. Worse for the wear, the men were stationed in the darkness to commence the attack at first light. According to some accounts, when the dawn's light first rose, it became clear that the paintings on the tipis belonged to Heavy Runner's camp. Mountain Chief must have heard rumors of the planned attack and switched camp location with that of the "friendly" chief, known as "peace" chief at the time. When Kipp again approached Baker with the error, Baker is reported to have replied, "That makes no difference, one band or another of them: they are all Piegans [Pikunis] and we will attack them." He then went on to direct one of his men to "stand behind this scout, and if he yells or makes a move, shoot him."[12]

When the first shots were fired, Heavy Runner emerged from his lodge, waving a piece of paper in his hand—an order of safe conduct issued by General Sully. Gunsmoke filled the air as round after round were fired. A total of 173 people were killed, most still in their lodges. The soldiers collapsed the lodges and burned them with the people inside. They gathered up the food, weapons, and supplies, and took them back to Fort Shaw, driving the Pikunis' horse herd in front of them. Baker falsely reported that all but fifty-three of the dead were "able-bodied warriors." W. A. Pease, the Indian Agent, reported to Baker's superiors that only fifteen of the dead had been fighting men, between the ages of twelve and thirty-seven. Ninety of the victims had been women, and fifty were children. Perhaps the rest were elderly people, although the account stays silent on that matter.[13]

The Blackfeet, Piegan, and Pikuni never again raised arms against the United States.

Conflicting reports did little to hide the horror of what had transpired. When the eastern newspapers got hold of the casualties, a great debate rose. Eastern sentiment was horrified, but closer to the events in Montana Territory, the view held that the attack had been justified and necessary. The US Army mounted an internal investigation. In the end, Sheridan and Baker were found not guilty of any wrongdoing. Baker became derisively known as "Piegan" Baker and did not receive a promotion for his actions.

Plagued by what appears to be alcoholism, his career fizzled. He was so drunk while overseeing a party of surveyors at Pryor's Fork in August 1872 that contemporaneous accounts reported him as unaware that a battle with the Sioux even raged around him. Paul McCormick,

A family grave scaffold.
LIBRARY OF CONGRESS. RICHARD THROSSER, PHOTOGRAPHER, C. 1905

a civilian freighter who had accompanied him on the Marias was again present on the Yellowstone attack. He recalled, "At this fight he [Baker] had 800 men, but if it had not been for the 'hangers on,' for whom he did not have much respect, he would have been whipped."[14] Unable to realize the enormity of the situation at the time, Baker emerged physically unscathed, but his health began to fail from 1873 onward. On December 18, 1881, he died at the age of forty-seven. The cause of death was given as "disorder of spleen and liver, splenic pain and jaundice."[15] All of which are symptoms of alcoholism.

FORT WHOOP-UP

In the 1850s, a road developed along the old Indigenous route called the Great Northern Trail, which had been used for a millennium. On the eastern side of the Rocky Mountains, parts of the trail were used for commerce between Fort Benton and southern Alberta, Canada. The origins of the name Whoop-Up remain unclear. Originally the name may have referred to the process of getting a bull train to move over a trail, a process called "whooping them up." A bull whacker would walk alongside the train, cracking his whip and thus providing the name.[16] A more popular option centers around the whiskey traded and the illicit activities that occurred along the 240-mile stretch of trail, where whoop-up refers to the raucous events whiskey fueled.

Fort Hamilton was the first fort built on the Canadian end of the Whoop-Up Trail in 1869, which conveniently coincided with Montana's enforcement of prohibition. Americans took their whiskey supplies and traveled up to Canada where they could continue their trade as they saw fit. The first fort burned to the ground due to an overturned lamp. A second construction occurred, taking two years. This time the completed fort was formally named Whoop-Up and opened for business in 1870. Selling a concoction called Whoop-Up bug juice, the "juice" consisted of alcohol spiked with ginger, molasses, red pepper, and colored with tobacco. It would then be boiled down to make "firewater." Such trade certainly contributed to the region's destabilization.

One such account where the blame could reasonably be laid on the whiskey trade came in the guise of the Cypress Hills massacre. This event occurred in 1873, again with several conflicting fundamental facts, even including whether the events took place in Montana or Canada. Regardless, the most coherent interpretation boils down to a party of men on their way from Fort Whoop-Up to Fort Benton who killed thirty-eight North Assiniboine just over the Canadian border. A seemingly objective account provided by Canadian Donald Graham documents his passage south along with a party of "wolfers." Along the way, twenty-two of their horses were stolen. In their attempts to recapture their stolen horses, they gave chase. Upon nearing Farwell's trading post, the party came upon a large Native encampment and were convinced their horses were not there. However, a cook from the camp approached the men claiming that the encampment held one of *his* horses, that they refused to return, and would someone in the party of wolfers help convince the tribe to give it back. Unwisely, the men agreed. The Assiniboine took exception, according to Graham's account, and fired first upon the wolfers. Armed with flintlocks, the Assiniboine were no match for the Winchesters of the wolfers. One wolfer was killed in the ensuing fight, and Graham claimed to have counted thirteen dead Assiniboine. The Canadian government charged fourteen men with having "shot down forty Indians in cold blood."[17] Three men would stand trial and were freed. The remaining men refused to return to Canada and were not extradited.

Graham claimed, "If blame can be attached to anything, this no doubt regrettable affair should be charged against the liquor traffic, at that time in full swing. The general opinion was that the Indians would never have attacked so quickly had they been perfectly sober."[18]

The whiskey trade reportedly ended with the arrival of the North-West Mounted Police in 1874, although alcohol abuse certainly did not.

CHAPTER 9

A TROUBLED HISTORY
SPILLS OVER

THROUGH THE LONG REACH OF HISTORY, IT IS INDISPUTABLE THAT THE Seventh Cavalry played a major role in western expansion and settlement of the territories and later, states. The entire US Cavalry and Infantry had a huge task placed in front of them. Their outlined duties centered around protection—keeping the roads and routes open, protecting settlers and travelers from hostiles (not just tribes, but also robbers and thieves, often called *road agents*), maintaining the telegraph wires, and acting as a general peacekeeping force, which also involved hosting negotiations. After the Civil War, the amount of traffic heading west across tribal lands *protected by treaty* lead to violence. A type of guerilla warfare ensued, characterized by skirmishes, pursuits, massacres, raids, expeditions, battles, and campaigns.[1]

The Battle of Greasy Grass (The Little Bighorn)

Chicago, Ill., July 7, 1876–1.10 a.m.

General P. H. Sheridan, U.S.A.,
    Continental Hotel

The following is General Terry's report, received late at night, dated June 27:

Custer's battlefield. Lettering the headboards. Photograph shows a man putting letters on a wood cross reading: "J. J. Crittenden, Lieut. 20 Infty." Cross marks the grave of Lieutenant John Jordan Crittenden III (1854–1876), who died at the Battle of the Little Bighorn.

"It is my painful duty to report that day before yesterday, the 25th instant, a great disaster overtook General Custer and the troops under his command. At 12 o'clock of the 22nd instant he started with his whole regiment and a strong detachment of scouts and guides from the mouth of the Rosebud; proceeding up that river about twenty miles he struck a very heavy Indian trail, which had previously been discovered, and pursuing it, found that it led, as it was supposed that it would lead, to the Little Big Horn River. Here

he found a village of almost unlimited extent, and at once attacked it with that portion of his command which was immediately at hand. Major Reno, with three companies, A, G, and M, of the regiment, was sent into the valley of the stream at the point where the trail struck it. General Custer, with five companies, C, E, F, I, and L, attempted to enter about three miles lower down. Reno, forded the river, charged down its left bank, and fought on foot until finally completely overwhelmed by numbers he was compelled to mount and recross the river and seek a refuge on the high bluffs which overlook its right bank. Just as he recrossed, Captain Benteen, who, with three companies, D, H, and K, was some two (2) miles to the left of Reno when the action commenced, but who had been ordered by General Custer to return, came to the river, and rightly concluding that it was useless for his force to attempt to renew the fight in the valley, he joined Reno on the bluffs. Captain McDougall with his company (B) was at first some distance in the rear with a train of pack mules. He also came up to Reno. Soon this united force was nearly surrounded by Indians, many of whom armed with rifles, occupied positions which commanded the ground held by the cavalry, ground from which there was no escape. Rifle-pits were dug, and the fight was maintained, though with heavy loss, from about half past 2 o'clock of the 25th till 6 o'clock of the 26th, when the Indians withdrew from the valley, taking with them their village. Of the movements of General Custer and the five companies under his immediate command, scarcely anything is known from those who witnessed them; for no officer or soldier who accompanied him has yet been found alive. His trail from the point where Reno crossed the stream, passes along and in the rear of the crest of the bluffs on the right bank for nearly or quite three miles; then it comes down to the bank of the river, but at once diverges from it, as if he had unsuccessfully attempted to cross; then turns upon itself, almost completing a circle, and closes. It is marked by the remains of his officers and men and the bodies of his horses, some of them strewn along the path, others heaped where halts appeared to have been made. There is abundant evidence that a gallant resistance was offered by the troops, but they were beset on all sides by overpowering numbers. The officers known to be killed are General Custer; Captains Keogh, Yates, and Custer, and Lieutenants Cooke, Smith, McIntosh, Calhoun, Porter, Hodgson, Sturgis, and Reilly, of the cavalry. Lieutenant Crittenden, of the Twelfth Infantry, along with Acting Assistant Surgeon D. E. Wolf, Lieutenant Harrington of the Cavalry, and Assistant Surgeon Lord are missing. Captain Benteen and Lieutenant Varnum, of the cavalry are slightly wounded. Mr. B. Custer, a brother, and Mr. Reed, a nephew, of General Custer, were with him and were killed. No other officers than those whom I have named are among the killed, wounded, and missing.

It is impossible yet to obtain a reliable list of the enlisted men killed and wounded, but the number of killed, including officers, must reach two hundred and fifty. The number of wounded is fifty-one. The balance of report will be forwarded immediately."

R. C. DRUM,
    Assistant Adjutant-General

P. H. Sheridan,
    Lieutenant General[2]

The blood-drenched events on June 25 and 26, 1876, rocked the nation. The official telegram provided a narrative that simply wasn't "supposed" to have happened. To this day, starting back to when the news became public knowledge, the Battle of the Little Bighorn has proven a watershed event in the history of the United States. Debates continue to rage as to whether Lieutenant Colonel Custer led his men to slaughter through arrogance and ambition, whether Major Marcus Reno proved drunk to the point of incapacity, and whether Captain Frederick Benteen—a vocal and harshly critical opponent of Custer's—could have done more to prevent the annihilation of Custer's men.

The only thing certain is that the Seventh Cavalry faced a superior fighting force: superior in numbers, determination, and organization. The overwhelming victory for the tribes was led by such noted warriors and chiefs as Sitting Bull, Crazy Horse, Gall, Lame White Man, and Two Moon. Beyond the army accounts of the horrific and resounding defeat of the Seventh Cavalry is testimony provided by tribal combatants who witnessed events and lived to tell about them. Their accounts claimed that soldiers shot pointlessly into the air, acted as if drunk, and even committed suicide upon approach. The supposed suicides may have resulted from the prevailing practice of saving the last bullet for oneself as a means of avoiding capture, scalping, or torture. Unfortunately, in their understandable terror, some of the soldiers may have resorted to that drastic means. The warriors who saw such actions didn't understand them, and some even said that the soldiers had a chance of survival, had they fought.

Like most everything about the actual fight of the Little Bighorn, even eyewitness accounts remain subject to interpretation and disagreement.

> *The soldiers charged the Sioux camp about noon. The soldiers were divided, one party charging right into the camp. After driving these soldiers across the river, the Sioux charged the different soldiers [i.e., Custer's] below, and drive [sic] them in confusion; these soldiers became foolish, many throwing away their guns and raising their hands, saying, "Sioux, pity us; take us prisoners." The Sioux did not take a single soldier prisoner but killed all of them; none were left alive for even a few minutes. These different soldiers discharged their guns but little. I took a gun and two belts off two dead soldiers; out of one belt two cartridges were gone, out of the other five.[3]*

Black Elk noted that "the soldiers were moving oddly. They were making their arms go as though they were running, but they were only walking."[4]

The US soldiers Black Elk referred to might have been wounded—with exaggerated arm movements to help propel themselves to comparative safety. Or it is possible that their minds played tricks on them in the hot sun and, likely suffering from severe thirst, may have had delusions.

Gen. George Custer

The Indians hunted them all down. The Oglala [sic] Brings Plenty and Iron Hawk killed two soldiers running up a creek bed and figured they were the last white men to die. Others said the last man dashed away on a fast horse upriver toward Reno Hill, and then inexplicably shot himself in the head with his own revolver.[5]

The man riding the fast horse that Black Elk referred to may have been Lieutenant Harrington, who rode a distinctive sorrel mount. Now the source of updated scholarship, it seems possible that Harrington, already wounded, may have leaned forward to shoot around his horse's neck and the overheated weapon exploded, giving the appearance that he killed himself. Or he might have put a bullet through his brain, but by many accounts, he had almost escaped to safety when his death occurred.[6]

Outmanned and outfought, the resounding loss of this battle (referred to as Custer's Massacre in earlier times) proved a massive but fleeting victory for the Lakota Sioux, Northern Cheyenne, and Arapaho.

While the maneuvers, personal grievances, and outcomes are well-known, an in-depth study is beyond the scope of this book. It is, however, worth looking into the impact the battle had on the survivors, and what became of their lives after that pivotal day. As is often the case, the officer's fates and those of their wives and children received far more attention than did those of the NCOs and enlisted men. As a case in point, Elizabeth Custer championed the plight of the widows in an attempt to alleviate hardship. As the widow of Lieutenant Colonel George Armstrong Custer, she waged a public campaign to rehabilitate her husband's tarnished reputation—a task she devoted the rest of her life to pursuing and defending. She remained constantly in the public eye, ever championing his cause.

As for Major Reno, he performed poorly at the Little Bighorn, as history attests. Nevertheless, after the battle he was assigned command of Fort Abercrombie in the Dakota Territory in 1876. At that post he became infatuated with the wife of another officer—the wife of Captain James M. Bell. He made unwanted advances toward Mrs. Bell. Perhaps his erratic actions were due to his tertiary syphilis. On May 8, 1877, a general court martial was held in St. Paul, where Reno was found guilty of six out of seven counts. He was dismissed from the army but was reinstated two years later by President Hayes.

Responding to the charges of cowardice and drunkenness at the Battle of the Little Bighorn, he asked for, and received, a court of inquiry, which exonerated him from those charges. However, the court of public opinion was not so kind in all instances, and especially not where Elizabeth Custer was concerned.

In 1879 Reno went on to command Fort Meade, again in the Dakota Territory. There he was court martialed again—this time on the charges of conduct unbecoming an officer due to a physical assault against a subordinate officer. He was dismissed from the service on April 1, 1880. He would spend the rest of his life in Washington, D.C., where he pursued the restoration of his military rank.

He remarried in 1882 to Isabella Steele Ray McGunnegle of New York City, the widow of Lieutenant Commander Wilson McGunnegle. The marriage failed, and a divorce followed in 1889.

Major Marcus Reno died from cancer of the tongue on March 30, 1889, at the age of fifty-four.

In 1926 the suggestion was ventured that Major Reno might have a monument at the Little Bighorn, but Elizabeth Custer did her best to block that honor. She was successful while still alive, but in 1967 Reno's remains were reinterred at the Custer National Battlefield, with honors.

Frederick Benteen conducted himself well and kept a level head as the battle raged at the Little Bighorn. The primary criticism leveled at him was his delayed response to Custer's request for assistance—a delay that likely saved lives in his command, possibly at the expense of Custer's. The argument is subject to conjecture. He took over for an incapacitated Major Reno. It is true that Benteen did not like Custer. What is not known is whether personal animosity caused the delay. Perhaps it is closer to the truth that Benteen could see that he was needed on Reno's line, with Custer's annihilation a near certainty.

Benteen served in the US Cavalry another twelve years after the Little Bighorn. Alcohol featured in his career afterward. While he was promoted, he was also disgraced. Charged with drunk and disorderly conduct in Fort Duchesne, Utah, in 1887, a military tribunal convicted him as charged. He faced dismissal from the army, but President Cleveland reduced his sentence to a one-year suspension. He retired in 1888 citing rheumatism and heart disease. Benteen died of natural causes in 1888 at the age of sixty-three.

THE DEAD AND THE WOUNDED AND A GHASTLY TASK

The immediate concern in the aftermath of the battle was the transportation of the wounded men for treatment. The steamer *The Far West* was pressed into service. Beyond rendering what assistance could be offered for the wounded men, burial details were arranged for those past assistance. The exhausted men under Reno's command were assigned to the horrific task, although other men assisted with the gruesome burials. The interments were hasty affairs, often little more than tin plate–scraped dirt and uprooted scrub tossed over the corpses. It's impossible to comprehend the impact this had on the men—surviving such a horrific battle and then being tasked to deal with the dead. "The bodies had lain in the hot June sun for over two days and were bloated and blackened due to exposure and the natural process of decay. The stench was unbearable, and the mutilation of the bodies must have added to the emotional trauma of the moment."[7]

Captain Walter Clifford, from the 7th Infantry, wrote in his journal:

Our camp is surrounded with ghastly remains of the recent butchery. The days are hot and still, and the air is thick with the stench of the festering bodies. . . . A brooding sorrow hangs like a pall over our every thought.

The repulsive-looking green flies that have been feasting on the swollen bodies of the dead are attracted to the camp fires by the smell of cooking meat. They come in such swarms that a persevering swing of the tree branch is necessary to keep them from settling on the food. . . . Let us bury our dead and flee from this rotting atmosphere.[8]

Because of the hurried nature of the initial burials, reinterments occurred in 1877, 1879, and 1881. During the reburials, the body of Lieutenant Harrington was not located, and therefore remained listed as missing.

To study the underlying effects of the Battle of the Little Bighorn on the survivors is a difficult task. In the 1870s, mental health concerns were typically viewed as "cowardice, character loss or lack of patriotism."[9] It is understandable, given the prevailing opinion at the time, that people displayed a great deal of caution when approaching anything that might have hinted at mental instability. Instability that came as the result of witnessing the carnage of an absolute slaughter.

Many of the soldiers also had underlying physical conditions even before the battle. At least nineteen of the men had syphilis, including Major Reno. Tertiary syphilis often impacted behavior as possibly witnessed by Reno's erratic actions later in his army career, including his performance during the battle of the Little Bighorn. Perhaps more concerning than what was then termed "syphilitic insanity" was the previous combat experience and trauma stemming from the Civil War. Of the 640 men who fought on the US side during the battle, 110 had fought in the Civil War, with nineteen of those sustaining injuries and battle wounds.[10] Reno himself had fought in the Civil War and participated in many battles, including Antietam. Some have written that Reno participated in over twenty engagements. It is possible that the trauma of those fights, combined with Bloody Knife's brains splattering over him at the Little Bighorn, unhinged Reno.[11] The viciousness of the unfolding slaughter might have caused something within him to snap.

Officers weren't the only combatants struggling. One of the men, Stanislas Roy from France, wrote an account of a man named Cornelius Cowley, a stonemason from Ireland who fought at the Little Bighorn in the valley and hilltop fights. Roy claimed, "Cowley went insane from thirst and did not recover for some time. We had to tie him fast on June 26."[12]

The unbalanced trooper suffered from ailments associated with the battle for the rest of his life. Roy wrote: "Cowley believed his attack of heart disease was due to over fatigue and exhaustion and the overpowering effect from the vast number of corpses both human and animal, in various states of decomposition and putrefaction lying on the field during and after the battle." Cowley died in a hospital for the insane in 1908.[13]

STARK STATISTICS

The enrollment of the Seventh Cavalry as it stood on the day of the Little Bighorn reveals notable information. This is what we know about the 817 names on the Seventh Cavalry roster of 1876:

Sick (unavailable for active duty day of battle): 27 men or 3 percent of the total fighting force.

Deserted: 1.

On Detached Service (4 men were en route to the post): A sobering 212 men were listed in this category and unavailable to assist/fight during the battle, equating to 26 percent of the fighting force. Detached duty or service occurred when the soldier/officer was assigned to service at another location. Those assignments could range from days to months in duration.

Medal of Honor recipient—24 men or 3 percent of those involved in the Little Bighorn battle.

Died at the Little Bighorn—272 or 33 percent.

Deemed Insane—John J. Fay (dismissed for insanity).

In Confinement (the brig/military jail)—13 men or 2 percent.

Details Concerning Offense—1 for liquor on Sunday.

Deaths on the Steamer the Far West—4 wounded men.

Died of Wounds—Frank Braun, Oct. 4, 1876, Fort Lincoln DT.

Straggler from Custer's column—1.[14]

The battle and subsequent burials obviously strained men past the breaking point.

Eleven troopers deserted in the last five months of 1876, some almost as soon as the bodies were buried and in the thick of Indian Country, according to a compilation of soldiers' histories. . . . William Channel and Edler Nees deserted on July 26 near the Bighorn River. Channel was caught the same day, and Nees, two days later. Both were placed in irons and sent back to forts in North Dakota where they were court-martialed and dishonorably discharged on Oct. 30, 1876.[15]

Survivors of the battle were likely haunted the rest of their days. A look into the next ten years shows a pattern of difficulty. Not all of the men mustered out, and some went on to fight further engagements against the Nez Perce and at Wounded Knee. See appendix B for a list of men who died within ten years of the Little Bighorn.

CROW AND ARIKARA (REE) SCOUTS

Scouts and interpreters played a critical role before and during the battle, fighting alongside the US Cavalry. Tribal history and conflicts played out all over the West. In the northern plains, the Ojibwe of the Great Lakes region pushed the Sioux out and further west. The displaced Sioux migrated into Arikara, Pawnee, Crow, and Shoshone territories. At the time of the Little Bighorn, the Sioux actively and willfully encroached upon prime Crow territory. During the smallpox epidemic of 1831, an inoculation program took effect among the Yankton, Yanktonai, and Teton Sioux that increased their survival rates, especially during the massive 1837 smallpox outbreak. Tribes further up the Missouri River were unvaccinated, suffering high mortality rates during epidemics as a result. In December 1862, the Sioux burned a large Arikara village, known as Like-a-Fishhook. The Arikara enlisted in the US Army to fight the Sioux in 1868 as a means of settling scores.[16]

Smaller tribes could only fight and defend against the Sioux if they had strong allies. The US government filled that role well, from a tribal perspective. The Pawnee were related to the Arikara. The Shoshone had been enemies of the Crow, but as the Blackfeet pushed them off the plains, they turned their hostility toward the Sioux, Cheyenne, and Arapahoe. The US Army became an ally by default. By the mid-nineteenth century, the Crow were locked in a battle of survival against the Sioux. As author Collin G. Calloway so brilliantly phrases it, "the Crows employed the United States as allies in their war for survival."[17]

As for early deaths of the scouts, Stab died in 1882 in Badlands Territory; again there are different accounts of his death. One reported he died as the result of a drunken brawl. Better documented is that Stab (also referred to as *Stabbed*) was shot by a Dakota during a raid upon Arikara horses and died as a result.[18]

After the Little Bighorn, tribal hostilities continued.

One of the more poignant stories involving the widows of the slain men concerns a troubled woman named Grace Berard Harrington. She was the wife of Lieutenant Henry Harrington, whose remains were missing in the aftermath of the slaughter. The reburial parties did not locate his remains either. Because of the failure to locate a corpse, Mrs. Harrington held on to hope. Becoming obsessed with the idea that her husband remained alive and held in captivity by the Sioux, she pleaded with officials to mount an expedition for his recovery. The powers in charge, believing her husband to be dead, did not pursue her requests. After being nearly incapacitated by grief, Grace Berard Harrington disappeared. Her daughter, Grace Allison Harrington, later explained "Several times we heard from Indians that a lady dressed in black had been seen on the battlefield. Other reports came from Indian Territory."

After two years, the widow Harrington resurfaced in Texas after suffering from amnesia and was reunited with her family. She was never able to give an account of her wanderings.[19]

The mystery of what happened to Lieutenant Henry Moore Harrington would never be solved during her lifetime.

In 2006, however, a skull was discovered in a box of the Smithsonian's anthropological holdings. That skull would be identified as belonging to Lieutenant Harrington.[20] And how did Lieutenant Harrington's skull end up in the Smithsonian labeled as "Army Medical Museum Specimen 2021"? Assistant Surgeon Robert Shufeldt, as part of a detachment from Fort Laramie on July 4, 1877, located Lieutenant Harrington's remains on the field—quite possibly with the assistance of a scout named War Club. The Surgeon General had directed medical officers to collect skeletal remains, and in particular skulls. In what was, no doubt, a serious breach of protocol, Shufeldt would not turn Harrington's skull over until 1882. Perhaps in exchange, he received an honorary curator position for the Smithsonian Institute. He would eventually go on to pen an account titled "Personal Adventures of a Human Skull Collector." Some of his relatives deemed him as actually insane.[21]

The impact of the Battle of the Little Bighorn would prove to have a long reach and impact lives for many years to come.

CHAPTER 10

SHADY LADIES AND THEIR EQUALLY SHADY MEN

In Montana during the 1860s, everyone chased after gold in one form or another, and the phrase "mining the miners" was no accident. Montana's first census, conducted in 1870, returned a population count of 12,418 males to 6,935 females between the ages of eighteen and forty-five, which certainly meant there weren't enough dance partners to go around! Enterprising women of the flesh trade saw the obvious, lucrative niche in the marketplace. The thing about shady ladies that remains widely overlooked to this day is that they were often significant economic powerhouses on the frontier. Derided, shunned, and viewed with disdain in general, these women might have been labeled "frail sisters," but most of them were anything but. Wielding a fair amount of economic prowess, albeit outside the bounds of acceptable society, these women added to the settlement's fabric in the West. Their exploits and sad, often violent lives were commented upon in the newspapers and held up for inspection and remark—with much of it unkind.

How these ladies of the underworld were viewed, tolerated, or even admired, depended largely upon the scarcity of women in a particular area, the availability of "honest women," and the individual's personal perception. Thomas Dimsdale, the rather stodgy newspaper scion of Virginia City, described them with a measure of kindness, even if he was wary of their workplaces. He provided this literary sketch of early Montana entertainment:

> One "institution," offering a shadowy and dangerous substitute for more legitimate female association, deserves a more peculiar notice. This is the "Hurdy-Gurdy" house. As soon as the men have left off work, these places are opened, and dancing commences. Let the reader picture to himself a large room, furnished with a bar at one end—where champagne at $12 (in gold) per bottle, and "drinks" at twenty-five to fifty cents are wholesaled (correctly speaking)—and divided, at the end of the bar, by a railing running from side to side. . . . Beyond the barrier sit the dancing women, called "hurdy-gurdies," sometimes dressed in uniform, but, more generally, habited according to the dictates of individual caprice, in the finest clothes that money can buy, and which are fashioned on the most attractive styles that fancy can suggest.[1]

In fact, much of Dimsdale's entire chapter is devoted to the hurdy-gurdy institution, dancing women, overpriced alcohol, and how crimes committed were judged and settled by miners' courts. It is unlikely that many of the "girls" were brought before actual miners' courts, but it would be possible on charges of theft or murder. When the legal establishment finally took hold, there were plenty of fines and charges for "drunk and disorderly" to go around.

One interesting, albeit later, opinion expressed about the profession of these women was offered by Teddy Blue Abbott, in reference to the relationships between cowboys and the girls for hire.

> I suppose those things would shock a lot of respectable people. But we wasn't respectable and we didn't pretend to be, which was the only way we was differed from some others. I've heard a lot about the double standard, and seen a lot of it too, and it don't make any sense for the man to get off so easily. If I'd been a woman and done what I done I'd have ended up in a sporting house."[2]

As families moved into the mining towns, meaning respectable women became more prevalent, a measure of the freewheeling air dissipated. In Virginia City, a demimondaine unlikely named Ranche Belle stole "three silver half dollars." She was later mentioned in the newspaper again; this time being fined $5 and costs for using "indelicate and disgusting language."[3]

Apparently, refinement drifted in the air. One resident of Virginia City even went so far as to write the following to the editor of the *Montana Post*:

EDITOR POST: Why don't you pitch in to that infernal nuisance on Jackson Street, called by some a dance house? I live a few doors down from it, and nearly every night my rest is broken by the shouts of drunken prostitutes and their partners. Sometimes the tumult lasts until morning, and it is high time this sink of infamy was removed. Fights are always occurring and dancers utter, hour after hour, the most obscene and profane remarks.

Yours in distress,
SUBSCRIBER[4]

From 1865 to 1883, speaking specifically of Helena, the "demimonde" was dominated by "proprietor prostitutes" who acquired their buildings— ranging in price from $600 to $1,000 paid for in either cash, or "good clean bankable gulch gold dust." Between 1865 and 1870, over $50,000 changed hands in property transactions.[5] One unique characteristic of this profession and location was the idea of more or less friendly competition. Many of the Helena madams worked together, although they were competitors. In this fashion, they formed a type of businesswomen's network far ahead of its era and time.

Enter Molly Welch, known as Mary Welch, also known as Josephine Airey, or Chicago Joe—an Irish woman with an eye toward making money. While her name might have been uncertain, one thing about her was not. The woman had plenty of ambition, and she had just rolled into the town of Helena.

Josephine Airey
WIKIPEDIA

The different names used by the famous madam Josephine Airey illustrates the difficulties involved with tracing individual histories of women. The goal of the game, if it could be called such, was to be the fresh face in town. Another name, a few years shaved off a declared age, and another location could do wonders (temporarily) for a woman's business prospects. "Fresh meat" is a common enough term, and although uncouth, it describes the situation accurately, especially for the boarders or the lodgers of the parlor houses and brothels. The madams themselves pursued a different business objective—namely, running a stable of workers—and while they might have pitched in occasionally with customers that needed servicing, they tended to possess a greater degree of stability with properties to manage and sizable businesses to run. All of which is not to say that they didn't pick up and move should the occasion warrant a change of scenery or if a new gold strike hit.

Josephine Airey, born in Ireland, was reportedly engaged in Chicago prostitution by the age of twenty-two.[6] Her illiteracy was countered by a sharp wit, strong business acumen, and the surprising ability to do math, and to do math well. She heard about the promise of the Montana gold camps from a Chicago gambler named Al Hankins, who himself viewed the territory with a professional interest.

Josephine arrived at Fort Benton in 1867 and made her way to the former Last Chance Gulch in April of that same year. There she found a rough settlement filled with muddy streets, rough log cabins and lean-tos, and an atmosphere teeming with activity. Immediately leaping into action, on April 5 she purchased a crude, single-story cabin on the former Bridge Street (now State Street) for $1,050. She started her operations out as the standard hurdy-gurdy house, where women sold dances for one dollar, and drinks purchased at a premium were strongly suggested after each and every dance. "Many unwashed customers arrived armed with pistols, drank to excess, and were hard, if not downright dangerous, to deal with."[7] Helena's good money, in those years, came only during the summer months. By winter, business slowed down considerably, and many prostitutes headed for more fertile hunting grounds. But the wealth in Montana proved something special. The "brides of the multitudes" would come back the following season—provided they were still alive and able. The cycle would repeat itself again with a couple of additions and a couple subtractions, with all the girls vying for gold.

Meanwhile, Josephine kept accumulating properties. Many of the other local madams, often referred to as *proprietor prostitutes*, made money hand over fist in that young, upstart mining district. The women were not shy about investing. This so-called easy money, and unusually generous natures concerning their tumultuous romantic attachments, made these madams attractive targets for a certain class of men.

As fate would have it, Josephine and Al Hankins—whose full flamboyant name is recorded as Prince Albert Hankins—crossed paths again. Al, it must be said, had a less than stellar reputation. He did, however, cut a fine figure of a man, if one managed to overlook the dubiousness of his character. Josephine, if she heard the rumors and the whisperings, ignored the warnings. She and Hankins wed in Helena on Valentine's Day in 1869.

While some accounts list a devastating fire in Helena that same day providing a more exciting story, the conflagration actually occurred on February 18, 1869,[8] and as such, did not mar the nuptials. Nevertheless, a combustible marital period followed. Apparently, the newlyweds headed out for the most recent strike in White Pine, Nevada, which didn't amount to much. Neither did their marriage. Al returned almost immediately to Chicago to build a gambling emporium in partnership with his brothers. Josephine returned to Helena with one less husband.

In the 1870s the "soiled doves" continued to arrive, now accompanied by increasing numbers of their less colorful sisters often referred to as "honest women." It is possible that public opinion and tolerance shifted away from the shady ladies. The territorial capital moved to Helena and as a result, the territorial legislature, yearning for respectability, tried to outlaw hurdy-gurdy houses and dancing emporiums to no avail. Saloons, dance halls, and brothels flourished. In an attempt to seize the upper hand, Ordinance No. 71 in Helena made women's employment on Main Street in any establishment selling intoxicating liquors a misdemeanor. Furthermore, it prohibited brothels on Main Street north of Bridge Street. Fines ranged from $1 to $100—irksome fines no doubt, but ones which the women considered little more than another cost of doing business.[9]

Despite attempts on curbing female vice, the 1870s ushered in a somewhat more professional age as far as the flesh trade was concerned.

In 1870, James T. "Black Hawk" Hensley traveled to Helena with the intent of becoming a professional gambler. As he honed his craft, he took up employment as a bartender and bouncer at Josephine's establishment. On October 1, 1871, Helena burned again—and again Josephine's establishment came through unscathed. She had largely managed to avoid mention in the newspapers. Considering her line of work, that proved a prudent precaution while it lasted. But a couple of instances were recorded of fights between Josephine and other "girls." On January 9, 1872, a newspaper reported: "One of the 'soiled doves' of Wood street, known as 'Chicago Joe' was up before Justice Totten yesterday for assault upon the person of Mollie Graham. She was fined $5 and costs."[10]

More detrimental was the following account:

> *A Democratic convention, at Helena, Montana, lately adjourned to witness a pugilistic encounter between a couple of irate amazons, "Chicago Joe" and the "Lady from the Bay." The floic [sic] damsels are otherwise known in biographical annuls as Annie Giessner and Josephine Ary [sic]. If there were no dog fight to ensue after the battle the convention intended to resume its deliberations.*[11]

Troubles still plagued Josephine, however, as was not uncommon on the margins of society. In 1873, hurdy-gurdy houses were deemed illegal under Montana law. Josephine simply changed the rules around. Dances were offered for free, but a drink had to be purchased beforehand, negating any benefit for the punter.

On January 9, 1874, Helena suffered yet another fire—but this time Chicago Joe's luck did not hold true. Her dance hall burned. On the other hand, her new romance Blackhawk, in the time leading up to the fire, had experienced a strong winning streak with his gambling. He bankrolled her new building, this time a dance hall constructed in stone. It was known as the Red Lantern.

Perhaps due to his display of generosity, or perhaps theirs was a true partnership, on December 17, 1878, Josephine and Blackhawk married. This time the marriage "took."

While other notable madams moved into Helena, such as Mollie Byrnes and Lillie McGraw, by 1883 Josephine remained the largest single property owner on Wood Street. That would make her the reigning Queen of the red-light district. Mollie Byrnes, also known as Belle Crafton, followed a close second and was no slouch. She built the brothel known as Castle in 1886, a lavish house by all accounts.

In September 1886 a crackdown occurred. Madams were accused of running hurdy-gurdy houses and brought before the courts. It seems, judging from newspaper reports, that such charges were easily side-stepped on technicalities. Josephine found herself likewise charged, but after all the legal wrangling and the fanfare the verdict came back as not guilty. That verdict, however, sparked plenty of editorial opinion on the plague of the hurdy-gurdies—one account going so far as to call such houses "the very hotbeds of hell."[12]

In 1887, Josephine opened a small variety theater called the Coliseum. Returns were good enough to warrant building a larger stone theater that was named the New Coliseum on July 4, 1888.[13]

Times were changing in Helena, as the city tried to shake off some of its former rough edges. In 1890, Josephine Airey found herself accused of selling liquor to a minor. On July 5, 1898, the following article was printed:

CHICAGO JOE'S GIRLS FINED

Seven women, inmates of the dance hall of "Chicago Joe" on Wood street, paid fines of $5 and costs each in the police courts yesterday. Complaint was made to the police by a man who said that he had been "rolled" and had $60 taken from him. Evidence could not be obtained to secure a conviction on the charge of robbery, but the women were arrested on the charges of being inmates of a dance hall and fined. They were booked as Alice Shelby, Lizzie Henry, Annie Adams, Gusele O'Brien, May Lawrence, Lena Dixon and Hattie Wade.[14]

Josephine Airey died from pneumonia October 25, 1899. No doubt it felt to many as if the end of an era had passed.

THE DARKER SIDE OF PROSTITUTION

No Wood Street woman before the mid-1880s had (remarkably) died of drug overdose or suicide, or at least no deaths were reported or labeled explicitly in the newspapers. But now such whitewashing of the prostitutes' lives, and circumstances, began to change. It was about this time when alcoholism, drug addiction, and suicide started to become a common occurrence in Helena. Mollie Byrnes, who built the Castle, might have had a more turbulent run at life than Josephine Airey, but nevertheless she decided to take a stab at middle-class respectability. Mollie chose for her partner Thomas Butler Eddingfield—a salesman at Feldberg's clothing store. The madam was thirty-two and Mr. Eddingfield twenty-eight when they married in 1890. On July 9, 1898, Mollie filed for divorce, claiming that her husband had repeatedly beaten her for the previous five years and that he had flung vile epithets at her, calling her "'low shanty Irish' and reflecting upon her chastity as a wife."[15] She further claimed that he had been the recipient of large sums of money from her, and due to his drunkenness, he proved unable to conduct business. The court found in Mrs. Eddingfield's favor, and on August 31, 1896, the marriage was terminated. As a final insult, Thomas Eddingfield failed to appear.[16]

Molly was not yet done with marriage. A month and a half later, on September 24, 1898, she married William "Willie" Weinsheimer, a supposedly wealthy sheep rancher from Marysville. However, for some unfathomable reason, she continued to see Eddingfield on the side. During February 1899, she got drunk with her former husband and sold him an undivided half-interest in her State Street building for $1.00. When everyone sobered up and he tried to file the bill of sale at the county clerk's office, Molly understood what she had done.

Back to court she went, this time charging Eddingfield with inducing her "to drink of drugged or intoxicating beverages until she became utterly incapable of doing business," which is when he convinced her to sell the property for $1.00. The court backed the woman. On December 11, 1899, she sold the Castle to John Steinbrenner, the owner of the Cosmopolitan Hotel, for $7,000. One year later, Mollie made Willie her sole heir, and three days later she died from acute alcoholism. Willie was finally a wealthy man.[17]

Suspicion swirled that Weinsheimer might have poisoned Mollie, but nothing was ever proven, although tongues certainly wagged.

THE CHINESE VICE COMMUNITY

Montana housed a community of Chinese prostitutes, but tracing information on them as a group provides challenges due to the tongs—originally Chinese associations providing legal, monetary, and protective services during the nineteenth century. The word *tong* meant "gathering place." However, as the century progressed, tongs also became organizations of secret societies or sworn brotherhoods often tied to criminal activity.[18] Due to widespread discrimination, those of Chinese descent often understandably preferred to solve matters among themselves. American law often failed them when needed or approached.

All prostitutes operated within a stratified society, whether of European, American, or Chinese descent. Regarding the Chinese prostitute, only a few Chinese prostitution contracts have been found, but they are heartbreaking. If the few examples are an indication of the norm, women were forced into terms that extended their contracted servitude for sickness, menstrual periods, or childbirth. Often these women were in fact, if not in name, slaves to the person who held their contract.

The higher-status Chinese prostitutes did not have sexual contact with western men, which would have been regarded as a form of pollution, thus lowering the woman's status and value among affluent Chinese men. Instead, these favored women occupied apartments or rooms and acted as hostesses, as well as providing companionship and sexual services for those same men. These women were reportedly well attired and able to accumulate some personal wealth within their arrangements.[19]

The lower rung of the Chinese prostitution hierarchy meant that women likely suffered through hellish conditions at twenty-five to fifty cents per assignation, with no viable or visible end in sight. These unfortunate women may have been sold into prostitution by their poverty-stricken families back in China. Upon arrival in the United States, these women's existences were a misery. Often, they occupied small rooms in opium dens, gambling halls, and other places where men might congregate. They were trapped in the American West with little hope for eventual freedom.

Chinese prostitutes had the associated strike of the opium trade tainting their reputations even further. Both levels of Chinese prostitutes were segregated from the other non-Chinese houses of prostitution.

Chinese prostitutes lived, nearly exclusively, in Chinatown, and thus near the community's opium dens. Chinese and Anglo-American prostitutes occasionally smoked opium in Chinatown. White prostitutes visited the dens with their friends from the demimonde. For Chinese prostitutes who smoked opium, the cost of the narcotic increased the debt they owed the men who held their contracts. Chinese and Anglo-American prostitutes used the drug for the same reasons that men chose to use it, a temporary escape from their lives or, possibly, a permanent exit through suicide.[20]

November 26, 1869
A little bit of a row occurred last night by some parties heaving rocks at a Celestial bagnio on Main street, and the occupants thereof returning the compliment with the contents of a six shooter. No damages. The location of these Chinese prostitutes on the public thoroughfares, is a nuisance. They have more brazen effrontery than the native-borns who take to retired streets. But it is questionable, at least, whether that method of banishing them is expedient. A general law against their location on main streets would drive nine-tenths of the Chinese from their present locations, and should be enacted.[21]

Prejudice and misunderstanding abounded.

In 1870, there were 660 Chinese men in and around Helena, of whom 452 worked in the placer mines, 56 were washermen, 31 were cooks or servants, 7 were gamblers, and 5 were saloon workers.[22] The remainder of the population worked at varying trades. No mention is made of females until 1880. In that census, there were only 19 Chinese women in Lewis and Clark County, and all but 2 listed as prostitutes. Of those two, one was listed as a wife, but the occupation of the other woman remains unknown.

What is known of these lives conducted on the fringes of society is that Chinatowns and the red-light districts were located in the same part of a town or city, and occupants of both were considered pariahs.

By 1902, the Chinese Exclusion Act had been enacted and the Chinese population in Helena fell.

Suicide, drug addiction, and alcoholism cut short many of the prostitutes' lives. Some have estimated that the average span of a working girl's tenure in "the trade" lasted little longer than five years. The demographics of the demimonde were varied, but certain aspects held true no matter which western location the woman plied her trade. The prime ages of a prostitute were between about fifteen and thirty years of age. One of the harsh realities of the prostitute's world was that age acted against them. This was a profession where a woman, provided she had not succumbed to disease or addiction, aged out. When a woman was deemed no longer attractive enough to earn a living selling her body, her other options evaporated. A "manager" or madam for younger women was a possibility if a woman had reasonable business sense and could persuade younger women to work for her. Also available were attendant positions as saloon keeper and abortionist.[23]

Suicide was attempted with notable frequency—a lamentable condition held up to ridicule by newspapers of the time. Often narcotics were the vehicle of choice: morphine, Rough on Rats, laudanum, and other concoctions usually achieved at least a close brush with death, if they failed in the ultimate aim. Take, for example, the sorry state of affairs experienced by Mrs. Lottie "Sorrel Mike" Ables Picket, first of Helena and later Butte. Obviously unstable and erratic, this unfortunate woman earned fame based upon her frequent suicide attempts. While the newspaper copy is not entirely clear, a portrait of a very rough evening emerges:

NEAR DEATH'S DOOR

Miss Lottie Pickett, suffering from severe [word lost] on Sunday afternoon last, took a dose of morphine, and not being relieved, took the [word lost] of the package, quantity unknown. Hough, being

summonsed at 8 o'clock in the evening, found the patient unconscious.
After three hours' work he succeeded in restoring her to consciousness,
and instructed her attendants not to permit her to sleep again. But
about midnight the doctor was again called and found his patient in
a profound stupor, from which she was not roused until about 4 a.m.
when she was pronounced out of danger.[24]

Lottie Ables Pickett died in 1881 from a gunshot wound to the stomach. Apparently when a customer did not pay for the wine he drank, she pulled a pistol, and he shot her in the stomach. Because of her previous suicide attempts, no mention is made of his identity, or if he was ever caught and questioned. While the newspaper listed her age as thirty, it was believed that she was only twenty-two.[25]

And who were these men who married the "public" women and at the very least lived upon their earnings, and at worst drove them to despair? They were often gamblers, former army officers, saloon keepers, and other men who populated the underworld. Often these men were content to let women support them, and the marriages or partnerships often proved violent and erratic.

The sad fact is, for all the money the women of the night fed into city coffers, most of them faded into obscurity. The saddest fact is that, in many instances, their true names were never even known.

CHAPTER 11

LAST CHANCE GULCH

MORE COMMONLY KNOWN AS HELENA TODAY, THE MONIKER LAST Chance Gulch conjures up all sorts of images, and most of them are true. But before last chances spring to mind, the origin of Helena brings up a string of firsts. In the summer of 1805, William Clark noticed an abundance of trails north of the Helena Valley used by the tribes for following the bison herds in their annual migrations.

> *Then they resumed their course along an old Indian road. In the afternoon they reached a handsome valley watered by a large creek both of which extend a considerable distance among the mountains; this they crossed and during the evening traveled over a mountainous country covered with sharp fragments of flint rock which bruised and cut their feet very much, but were scarcely less troublesome than the prickly pear of the open plains which have now become so abundant that it is impossible to avoid them, and the thorns are so strong that they pierce a double sole of dried buffalo hide. At night they reached the river much fatigued. . . . Captain Clark's first employment on lighting a fire, was to extract from his feet the briars, which he found to be seventeen in number.[1]*

Thus were the likely, and painful, origins of the naming of Prickly Pear Valley by western discoverers.

In 1853, the federal government commissioned surveys and studies on the northern Rocky Mountains for potential railroads. The most prominent of these surveyors was West Point graduate and lieutenant in the US Corp of Topographical Engineers John Mullan.[2]

Together he and the Washington Territorial governor lobbied Congress for funding—which they received. The plan was to build a military wagon road from Walla Walla to Fort Benton, which would cover a total of 624 miles. Construction began in 1859. In 1860, the road skirted the Helena Valley. In 1862 with the gold strike, the road provided a much-needed thoroughfare for miners and supplies required by the mining camps. The discovery of gold on Last Chance Gulch—an offshoot of Prickly Pear Creek—occurred in 1864. John Cowan, Bob Stanley, Gabe Johnson, and John Crab (known to history as the so-called Four Georgians) gave their fledgling mining camp the name "Last Chance." Their supposed last chance drew hundreds of miners by 1865 and the typical assorted cast of characters flowed into the Helena Valley by the following year. A new offshoot was blazed from Mullen Road to what would become Helena. Known as the Fort Benton Road, it traversed 130 miles from Helena to Fort Benton and provided stage stations or mile houses every ten to fifteen miles along the route. Some of those stage stations had shady reputations, but for the most part travelers could find a measure of rest and nourishment, as well as the ability to have horses, mules, and other livestock seen to. Before long, Last Chance Gulch became known as Helena by "popular vote" (well, at least seven self-appointed men made their decision) on October 30, 1864.

THE ORIGINS OF HELENA

The discovery of gold combined with the ease of access Mullan Road provided meant that Last Chance Gulch grew and prospered. False-fronted buildings sprung up along what was known as Old Bridge Street, so named for a bridge that crossed the creek at the base of the street.

On October 30, 1864, the rather crass name of Last Chance Gulch was changed to the more civilized Helena. At one point, some accounts named the settlement "Crabtown" in honor of one of the Four Georgians, John Crab. In any case, the origins of the naming of Helena are somewhat murky, ranging from Minnesota miners reminiscing about a Minnesota town bearing the same name to a variety of other tales. However, dividing along Civil War lines, the Confederates pronounced the

1870 photograph of the vigilante lynching of Arthur Compton and Joseph Wilson in Helena, Montana
WIKIMEDIA COMMONS. C. 1870. EXTRACTED FROM FREDERICK ALLEN, "MONTANA VIGILANTES AND THE ORIGINS OF 3-7-77," *MONTANA: THE MAGAZINE OF WESTERN HISTORY* 51 (SPRING 2001): 9.

name Hel-UN-na, while the Union sympathizers called it Hel-EE-na. Today, the common pronunciation may be the Confederate version, but on occasion people will refer to Hel-EE-na.

Strangely enough, in comparison with other early settlements in the territory, Helena wasn't served by newspapers until 1866. That may be one reason for the comparative dearth of early details for this gold camp. However, the other newspapers established in Virginia City cast a wary eye in the direction of the new upstart, and with good reason.

As a letter-writing correspondent recorded on February 7, 1865: "Helena, in Last Chance Gulch, will doubtless be a business center of no mean importance. It already has some 75 houses completed, and as many more commenced. . . . Yours Truly, TYRO."[3]

In 1867 the Four Georgians sold their claims for $40,000 and returned to the States, journeying to the Philadelphia Mint to cash in their three years of hard work. They might have sold too soon.

This was the first photograph of Helena, taken in 1865. Stand on South Park Street with the old federal building on your right and the library on your left. Look east toward State Street.
WIKIMEDIA COMMONS. MONTANA HISTORICAL SOCIETY IMAGE # 954–177

The Last Gulch district ended up claiming the second largest strike in Montana, producing a remarkable $19 million of gold. Most important, Last Chance Gulch would go on to become the Montana state capital.

As one writer described the fledgling town, "With its main stem jammed with ox-teams, men and merchandise, cabins and stores abuilding in frantic haste, rockers and sluice boxes lined with gold, saloons and hurdy-gurdys whooping it up and a fresh corpse dangling from a limb on Hangman's Tree, the Prickly Pear valley remained serene and unaltered."[4] Serene and unaltered it wasn't. Like all western gold camps, the heady mixture of miners, suppliers, liquor, gambling men, and mercenary women poured into the settlement. By March 1865, likely a thousand people inhabited the camp, and it is believed that number tripled by summer. Again, law and order took a turn toward vigilantism in 1865 with the formation of the Committee of Safety, in response to the frantic pace and the opportunistic behavior on the parts of some of the more dubious inhabitants.

As before, it was a mixed bag concerning the validity of the rough justice.

The common mixture of alcohol, tempers, hard feelings, and potentially theft or wrong doings in many cases prompted a return to vigilantism. In some cases, hangings were the result of barroom brawls. Between June 9, 1865, and April 30, 1870, there were approximately eighteen known executions.[5] Far less attention is paid to the executions in Helena than Bannack or Alder Gulch, perhaps because the hangings were spread out over a longer period of time. Without a doubt, vigilantism in Helena followed an individual-by-individual basis, without the shadow of an organized group of marauders. By the time vigilantism arrived in Helena, it was already an established practice and many people found it acceptable.

On Monday morning, the beams of the rising sun fell upon the stiffened corpse of Tommy Cooke, a thief, swinging in the breeze, with a fatal token of vengeance of the Vigilantes around his neck, and bearing on the label a simple legend "Pickpocket." Tommy Cooke was a thief and a rough "from the other side," whether Boise or California we know not: but the usual course of education embraces a residence in both of these training grounds of the Road Agents, robbers and desperados of the West. Cooke was probably a graduate of both places. A number of robberies were noticed in our last issue, and through the praiseworthy exertions of Deputy Marshal "Quill" Lawrence, the perpetrator was traced up, arrested and held for trial. A court that no finessing could deceive had determined the question of his fate. He was taken from the custody of his captors and the next time that he was seen, his career of crime had met with the appropriate termination.

The climate of Montana is unhealthy for criminals, and Helena seems to be particularly so.[6]

A brief rundown of the people and causes of the vigilante executions in Helena follows.

January 1865—Zacharia Fogarty was hanged in Helena while awaiting transport to Bannack for trial concerning a murder in Fort Owen.

June 8, 1865—John Keene murdered Harry Slater by shooting him in the head execution style at Sam Greer's Saloon. Keene gave himself up to a man named Charlie Curtis, who turned him over to Sheriff George Wood. Kept in Wood's house because no jail had yet been built, a mob of men forcibly removed him from the sheriff's house and organized a trial by jury. Some members of the jury had taken part in the Vigilance Committee in Virginia City prior to events in Helena, which did not bode well for Keene. The impromptu trial was adjourned so that witnesses for Keene's defense could be located—but whether witnesses actually came is up for debate, dependent upon the source. Keene was convicted unanimously and hanged on a large "weather-worn bull pine" in the direction of Dry Gulch. Keene's drop was not clean, and he strangled on the noose for twenty-three minutes before dying. John X. Beidler was the superintendent of the hanging.[7]

While this may or may not be considered vigilantism since a trial was conducted, this marked the origins of the Committee of Safety in absence of an effective court. Judge Lyman Munson had not yet arrived at the fledgling community but would soon arrive on July 9, 1865. He resigned in 1868, which is not surprising given the following events.

One month after Keene's hanging, Jack Silvie, also known as Jacob Seachrist, was captured in Diamond City, forty miles away from Helena. He was accused of robbery and "obtaining goods under false pretenses, and various other crimes of a kindred sort."[8] Silvie, at first, claimed to having joined the road agents in Virginia City, but later retracted that statement. Upon further questioning, so the story goes, he said that he had joined a band of robbers at the Columbia River, confessed to murdering one miner, and described how he had shot the man, tied him to a large rock, and threw him into the river. The man's corpse had been found by the same posse that located Jem Kelly.[9] When brought to the hanging tree, Silvie reportedly confessed to a dozen additional murders. He was intentionally not given a clean drop and was hoisted into the air to die of slow strangulation.

When Judge Lyman Munson arrived in Helena, reportedly one of his first sights was that of a man's corpse hanging on the hanging tree—presumably that of Silvie/Seachrist. He convened the first grand jury on August 12, 1865, but did not condemn the efforts of the vigilantes. Nor did the court ever bring charges against the Committee of Safety.

Our list continues.

September 11, 1865—saloon keeper J. Hineman was robbed while traveling on foot and shot. Four days later on September 15, Jack Howard was hanged in Diamond City for that crime.

September 18, 1865—Tommy Cook, an apparent pickpocket, was hanged on Helena's hanging tree.

October 3, 1865—Con Kirby was hanged from the same tree for unknown reasons.

October 7, 1865—the *Montana Post* reported that two men were hanged at the Prickly Pear Tollgate, names omitted.

October 1865—another unnamed man hanged at Confederate gulch. Details unknown.

November 21, 1865—George Sanders was hanged on the tree. A note pinned on his clothes said, "This man was hung for robbing A. Slane of $1,180 and for other small stealings."[10]

November 23, 1865—two unknown men hanged on Helena's hanging tree with no details.

February 5, 1866—a barroom brawl resulted in a stray bullet hitting an innocent German man named Fisher. Charles Jewitt was arrested by Sheriff Mendenhall but was seized and hanged by vigilantes.

March 2, 1866—James Daniels was hanged while in the possession of an official reprieve from the territorial governor, Tomas Francis Meagher.

March 12, 1866—Leander W. Johnson was removed from a sheriff's custody and hanged in Deer Lodge for having stolen cattle from Reese Anderson. The cattle eventually returned to Anderson's ranch; therefore, they were merely estrays. There is high probability this was a hanging of an innocent man.

April 20, 1866—J. L. Goones was hanged after having been convicted of stabbing High "Jack" Dowd, his mining partner. Dowd survived, but Goones was still hanged. Upon his death, Goones (who always wore a hat) revealed a branded forehead, reportedly a common punishment for petty crimes.

June 5, 1866—John "Frenchy" Crouchet hanged on the weight of circumstantial evidence possibly linking him to sluice box theft.

January 5, 1867—a vigilante poster printed in the *Montana Post* read:

In view of the fact that crime has run riot to such an alarming extent in the Territory of Montana (particularly east of the Missouri River) during the past six months, and that murders and high handed outrages have been of such frequent occurrence as to excite the just indignation of all good citizens, it is believed that now is the time that the good work should be recommenced. Therefore, this is to notify all whom it may concern, that crime must and will be suppressed; and, to that end, all offenders will be summarily dealt with, and punished as of old.

By Order of the Vigilance Committee[11]

October 22, 1867—J. M. Douglas was arrested for the theft of twenty-two head of cattle from men called Pelaux and LeBeau. He escaped but was recognized at Big Hole Station and apprehended along the Rattlesnake River. He offered to give Pelaux and LeBeau whatever property he owned to repay them but was nevertheless hanged on November 13, 1867, at Red Mountain City. One wonders if Douglas's offer was extended to the ranchers who lost the head of cattle.

January 30, 1868—two purported horse thieves named Spaulding and Billy Wilson were accused of stealing the horses from Thomas Reeves's ranch. On their way to Salt Lake City, descriptions were telegraphed ahead and James O'Connor located the men in question. One problem—the horses they rode did not match the description of the horses stolen. The rationale at the time was that the horses could have been exchanged for fresh mounts. A "vigilante trial" ensued, where Wilson feigned sickness, escaped, and later was recaptured. Spaulding was hanged on January 29 or 30 at the White Tail Deer Station. Wilson was hanged from a tripod of "three corral poles erected at a roadside for all to see" on January 30, 1868.[12] Because the ground was frozen at that time of year, eventually he was taken down, a hole was cut in the nearby Jefferson River, and his body was left to the effects of the water, and likely floated downstream.

May 18, 1868—George Ballou was executed for taking part in the stabbing death of Johnny Gordon outside of his saloon. Ballou's fate was determined by jury, with his trial taking place in a vacant building once used by the Lee & O'Connell Store. Again, one wonders where the established law was during these events.

August 13, 1868—vigilantes forcibly seized John Varley away from official law enforcement. Varley robbed a man named Julian Guezals at knifepoint. Guezals, born in Spain, had served in the US Navy, yet Deputy Sheriff Kane stated that "a white man did not deserve to be punished much for robbing a 'greaser.'"[13] The vigilantes located Varley, refused to turn him over to Kane, conducted a trial, and hanged him in Beartown (now a ghost town near Helena).

August 20, 1868—William Hinson was hanged by vigilantes from another "tripod gallows" for highway robbery.[14]

But vigilantism was not yet finished.

THE CHINESE IN HELENA

In the 1870s, the Chinese community was estimated at 10 percent of Montana's overall population and are believed to have made up a significant 20 percent of Helena's citizenry. Facing prejudice and curtailment of opportunity, the Chinese lived in a "China town" near the red-light district. Chinese arrived in Montana from other western mining states, and directly from China. As workers, the Chinese had the reputation of being hardworking, accepting lower wages than whites, of demonstrating success in gleaning riches from mine tailings, and successfully running businesses such as laundries, and later restaurants. Some of their successes attributable to their own hard work threatened Caucasian inhabitants, frequently struggling to survive themselves.

One strange account occurred in Helena in 1866 when previously established washerwomen complained of the economic threat the Chinese posed. On January 27, 1866, a letter was sent to the *Montana Radiator* from "a committee of ladies" who complained that the Chinese were preventing them from earning a living. The newspaper was started by a man named T. J. Favorite, and he wrote a poem championing the ladies' cause in what appears to be an Irish brogue:

> Chinamen, Chinamen, beware of the day,
> When the women shall meet thee in battle array!
>
> Ye hopeless professors of salsoda and soap,
> Beware the fates that await ye,
> No hangman's committee with ladder and rope,
> But the ladies are coming to bate ye.
>
> Ye almond-eyed leather faced murthering heathens'
> Ye opium and musk stinking varmints,
> We will not object to your livin' and breathin'
> But beware of the washing of garments.
>
> To stay or to go ye can do as you chose
> To us it don't make any odds
> So long as ye keep your hands off of the clothes
> And keep out of the lather and suds.[15]

In reaction to the laundry challenge, a group of Chinese men paid for a response in the newspaper.

GOOD CHINAMEN

This is to certify that we, the undersigned, are good Chinamen and have lived in California and other parts of the United States, and that we have at all times been willing to abide by all the laws of the United States, and the States and Territories in which we have lived. And are now willing to deport ourselves as good law-abiding citizens of Montana Territory, and ask but that protection that the liberal and good government of the country permits us to enjoy. We pay all our taxes and assessments, and only ask that the good people of Montana may let us earn an honest living by the sweat of our brow.

Ye Sing
Hob Hee
Ye Hob and others[16]

Somewhat predictably, Favorite made light of the men's response.[17]

From the late 1860s through the 1870s, the Chinese came to Montana to work on the railroads and often to mine. In 1874, this assumption of a right to work in mining would be challenged. The Montana Territorial Legislature passed a law providing for the forfeiture to the Territory of placer claims belonging to "aliens." No alien could possess an interest in a mining claim and profit from it. This act was aimed squarely at the Chinese (most of whom made their living by working previously abandoned mines). This exclusion was applied retroactively.

Fauk Lee, a citizen of China, had purchased 3,000 feet of placer mining ground from S. Stevens in direct conflict with the law. This case made it all the way to the Montana Territory Supreme Court. Lee prevailed.

Until the Chinese Exclusion Act became law in 1882, the Chinese citizens put their faith in Montana's established legal systems. However, like much of the rest of the country, in the mid-1880s Montana's courts became anti-Chinese as anti-Chinese movements swept across the western United States. The first Chinese Exclusion Act prohibited Chinese immigration for ten years. Over time, as the courts became more biased, a prevalent feeling was that the Chinese needed to understand the laws. For example, the Montana Supreme Courts ruled against Chinese litigants over the ownership of quartz-crushing equipment. A Chinese defendant named How had been defrauded by the First National Bank of Helena. The bank sold How title-disputed equipment. The justices felt that How should have known of, or understood, the risk and disallowed the fraud claim as a valid defense.[18]

BACK TO THE VIGILANTES

In January 1870 there came a dispute between a Chinese man named Ah Chow and John R. Bitzer. The details of what provoked the incident are unclear, but the result was the shooting death of Bitzer in Chow's cabin. Chow's wife, Jasmine, claimed that Bitzer had attacked her. Who held the gun that did the shooting remains unclear, as Chow, according to a doctor's testimony, had a disabled right arm that would have prevented him from shooting. Bitzer claimed before dying that he had come into the cabin to assist a woman (presumably Jasmine) in a domestic dispute because her husband was beating her. Chow disappeared after the shooting and a $600 reward was placed on his head.[19] Within a few days, Chow was caught by lawman John X. Beidler, who turned him over to the Committee of Safety, which again calls into question exactly how the law in Helena functioned. Chow was hanged on the hanging tree January 24, 1870. The sign pinned on his back read, "Ah Chow, the murderer of John R. Bitzer. Beware! The Vigilantes still live!"[20]

Beidler collected the $600, which some viewed as blood money. While some felt the hanging of Chow was justified, others held grave concerns that an innocent man was hung without due process of law.

On March 12, 1870—W. C. Patrick was hanged for the murder of John Benser, seized while in custody in Diamond City.

April 27, 1870—a double hanging took place for Joseph Wilson and Arthur Compton; the men had attempted to kill George Leonard (also referred to as George Lenharth) with the aim of stealing his money. Leonard had been drinking heavily in Joe Reed's saloon. When he left the saloon, he was chased on horseback to the Spokane Creek, where he was shot and left for dead. Leonard was able to describe the horses the men rode but not the men themselves. It is unclear whether the men received judicial trials. Some authors believe that because a picture exists of the hanging taking place in broad daylight, a trial must have been held—the thought prevailing that the cloak of darkness would help to hide the identities of the vigilantes.

More vigilante executions took place in the 1870s in the Montana Territory; however, it seems that such actions precluded Helena at the point in time.

TERRITORIAL CAPITAL AND WEALTH AND SUSPICIONS

In 1875, Montana's Territorial Capital moved from Virginia City to Helena.. The first Territorial seat had been Bannack in 1862, which moved to the populous Virginia City in 1865.

Shared Capital Duties

Already by that early point in Montana's history, the population shifted away from Virginia City and over to Helena. This shift marked the beginning of a competition to hold the prized designation of capital—a distinction that would go a long way toward guaranteeing the availability of jobs, commerce, and longevity. In 1867 a vote was taken as to where the capital should reside, and Virginia City succeeded. Then, as gold production decreased, Virginia City's vitality declined while Helena's grew. Another vote was taken in 1869, and amid widespread accusations of fraud, Helena succeeded. When the ballots were taken to the territorial secretary's office, a fire destroyed them. Accusations and suspicions circulated. Again, in 1874 the question was placed before voters, "for or against Helena." Again, irregularities surfaced. Gallatin County's votes were thrown out, Meagher County's votes were deemed fraudulent, and the US Supreme Court refused to consider the case on appeal.[21]

The Montana Territorial Supreme Court ruled in Helena's favor.

Helena had the advantage of lying on a proposed rail line, was centrally located, and was flanked by rich, producing mines.

Wealth

In 1888, Helena reportedly had more millionaires per capita than any other city in the world. There were fifty millionaires for a population of 12,000, which creates a slender percentage of .004 percent (less than 1 percent) of millionaires for the overall population.[22] One man who contributed mightily to that statistic was a man born in Cavan, Ireland— Thomas Cruse. Cruse arrived in Helena in 1867 but didn't make his strike for nine years. Tommy, as he was known, unsuccessfully started his mining career in California, then Idaho, and finally in Montana. Working along the banks of Silver Creek outside of Helena, he noticed how gold attached itself to quartz. Following that hunch, he struck what looked like a mother lode, only to have his shaft fill up with water. Keeping his discovery silent, he dug a drainage tunnel. As he burrowed away and kept silent, the other miners in the district believed he was mentally unhinged. However, his perseverance paid off in 1876. He discovered a rich ore ledge that had both silver and gold. Cruse named his strike Drum Lummon for his home parish back in Ireland.

Typical of his modest manner, his tunnel was only large enough for one man to crawl in, and none of his ores were milled until 1880.

In 1886 he got married at the age of fifty to Margaret Carter, the sister of former Montana Senator Thomas H. Carter. Unfortunately, Margaret died that same year, ten days after giving birth and leaving an infant daughter named Mary behind.[23] Called "Mamie," she was the only child of Thomas Cruse, who never remarried. Mamie lived a turbulent life, and died at age twenty-six in 1913, preceding her father to the grave by one year. She had married and divorced three times and succumbed to alcoholism. Her father brought her to the House of the Good Shepherd where the nuns took care of her for some weeks. Eventually she was released to her father's care but died a few days later. The cause on her death certificate was listed as Bright's disease—an ailment of the kidneys, although there was speculation about the true cause.[24]

BACK TO THE QUESTION OF CAPITAL STATUS

While final word on the location of Montana's capital may appeared to have been settled during 1874, this proved not to be the case.

The 1889 constitution left the debate wide open. The 1892 vote had not been a decisive victory in Helena's favor, so a runoff election in November of 1894 was posed to settle the issue. The contenders were Helena and Anaconda. W. A. Clark stepped forward as a proponent of Helena, and Marcus Daly, the founder of the town of Anaconda, unsurprisingly came forth as its champion. Both men were millionaires, and neither man took kindly to losing. The primary arguments ran along the lines that Anaconda was a company town that supposedly enjoyed a feudal hold over its workers. Anaconda slung mud over in Helena's direction by ridiculing its "airs and graces" and the black and Chinese populations of that city. Free booze came by the barrelful, parades were staged, and even free money occasionally floated around. It is believed that Daly spent over two and a half million dollars, and Clark spent four hundred thousand. The state returned just over 52,000 votes cast in the election. Helena won by just under 2,000 votes.[25]

As an interesting aside, it has been claimed that a house in Helena held a secret. When the owner of that house passed on, a box was found containing ballots. Those ballots cast in the 1894 election, when tallied, would have yielded vastly different results.

Montana's capital, had those votes been counted, would have fallen in favor of Anaconda.

CHAPTER 12

RETRIBUTION

1879–1890

As with the miners and early inhabitants of Montana's gold camps, the open range stockmen, or stock growers, were often the victims of thefts—this time it wasn't gold but horses and cattle.

And strangely enough to the modern ear, the term *rustler* didn't hold the same connotations that it does today. Originally in the West, *rustle* meant to make do or to secure in a vigorous way. By 1884, the definition morphed, with the word *rustle* being used as it is today, meaning to steal.[1]

With remarkable foresight, in 1864 the first Territorial Assembly held in Bannack tackled the topic of marks and brands, which would be the first step in establishing a brand registry or recording method. Despite the promising early start, the fledgling act didn't provide any means of enforcement for the protection laws. At that early date in the territory's history, the majority of stock came from emigrants. As there wasn't a large population, marks viewed or used locally would have been known and recognized. But the influx of brands did not guarantee their original provenance. Branded animals could have easily been stolen in other locations and ridden or driven into Montana without the slightest indication of foul play.

Mining camps and army posts created a strong demand for beef, and money was to be made in supplying cattle to those marketplaces. One of the primary constraints that the Montana market was forced to contend with was the lack of railheads. That lack of railheads meant there was no easy way to transport livestock either to or from markets other than the slow and difficult traditional cattle drives. In 1873, cattle were driven overland to the railhead in Granger, Wyoming—which took sixty days. The buyers of those cattle must have liked what they saw, because in 1874, the following year, buyers came from the East to Deer Lodge Valley and Virginia City, paying $18.00 to $22.50 per head. Noted Montana cattleman Conrad Kohrs claimed, "We marketed some magnificent cattle, my native three-year-olds usually weighed 1,300 to 1,350 on the Chicago market, far outweighing the triple wintered Texan."[2]

Kohrs is, of course, referring to Texas cattle and not the Texas cowboys.

The early cattle industry flourished in Deer Lodge Valley, where Kohrs had holdings. Reportedly Deer Lodge Valley contained an impressive 75,000 head of cattle, but ranching flourished in other parts of Montana as well. The number of cattle in Montana doubled between the years 1875 and 1880.[3]

When the cattle boom of the 1880s took off, so did crime on the rangeland.

In 1883, Montana cattle were valued at $25 million. According to some estimates, rustling losses stood at 3 percent, which was not an inconsequential amount of money.[4] Individual efforts among the ranchers to curtail rustling proved time-consuming, expensive, and ultimately not entirely effective. Livestock were driven over the border into Canada to sell or were taken out of the region into nearby states, localities that did not worry all that much about a variety of brands in the same shipment or herd.

Although violence was not unknown, the Montana ranchers preferred to work within the existing governmental and legal framework, opposed to outside of it.

From the earliest attempt to organize cattle in Bannack in the 1860s, the first documented meeting of ranchers took place in December 1873 in Virginia City. More meetings followed. A bill was presented in 1874 that split up counties into stock districts, mandated joint roundups, and appointed stock inspectors. Also addressed was the issue of strays, where it was suggested they be branded with the district brand and sold at auction to the highest bidder. The organization that drafted this bill did not survive, and no further attempt to organize was made until 1878. On July 11 of that year, twenty-two ranchers met and formed the Montana Stock Association of Lewis and Clark County. They called for legislation to inspect brands; they also petitioned for the hides of slaughtered animals to be available for public view to discourage the practice of venting (rebranding or altering) hides.

The incidents of range theft increased.

The stockmen held their first statewide meeting on January 23, 1879, convening in Helena. The Territorial Stock Association incorporated in July of that year. This group struggled due to suspicion or hesitancy as to what such an organization might accomplish for ranches in outlying areas. Still, two more organizations formed, and the notion of range and stock control strengthened. In 1881, small, localized organizations took root. By 1882, Montana stock organizations had become widespread throughout the state. Decentralized and without a common charter, such groups remained inward looking and lacked a unified response.

The rustling problem worsened.

At the thirteenth Legislative Assembly held in Helena in 1883, Joseph A. Baker from Chouteau County introduced a bill for the better protection of stock interests in the territory. Many of their initial propositions met with success. However, House Bill 49, which would have established a board of five commissioners along with six stock detectives holding the power of arrest without warrant, was defeated. At the heart of the defeat stood the proposed mill levy of one-third of a mill, meaning one-thousandth of a dollar on *all* the taxable property in the state. The bill unsurprisingly proved unpopular with the mining and farming interests, who had huge holdings that would now be penalized. The argument went against levying a tax for the betterment of one industry over the interests of other industries. Governor Crosby vetoed the bill as a result.

After the 1883 fall roundups, when stock tallies were taken and compared, the losses experienced over the previous six months became apparent and alarming. Perhaps the most shocking aspect of that tally was not the number of cattle that had been pilfered but rather the number of horses. Horses traveled fast and could be rapidly moved out of the country or territory with comparative ease. Large stock producer Conrad Kohrs was in favor of a plan to send out a regiment of cowboys—similar to the idea supported by Teddy Roosevelt and the Marquis de Mores of the Dakota Territory. Roosevelt and de Mores wanted to form an "army of cowboys" to string up every horse thief encountered. Whether this was an exaggerated concern or not, at that time there were few, if any, stockmen who had not fallen victim to the scourge of range thieves or "land pirates." Many of those ranchers who lost valuable property felt that something needed to be done to stop their losses.

And if legislation couldn't or wouldn't get the job done, they would take matters into their own hands.

Violence stalked the land, and newspapers were quick to fan the flames.

Story after story about rustlers were printed in the local newspapers. One gets the sense of the magnitude of the coverage—and the mounting violence—from the following account:

A NEBULOUS STORY

The following . . . telegram from Miles City is published in the St. Paul Day. Take it for what you think it is worth: the fight at Mingus-ville between cowboys and horse-thieves was hot. Five empty saddles belonging to cowboys were found on the field. The vigilantes are said to have come from Wyoming. If so, they are bent on vengeance. There were four of the party hanged on Beaver, 17 miles north of Mingus-ville, near Gries and Wauber's ranch. Ole Berg, who led one gang of cowboys, is the respected son-in-law of Judge Allen of Glendive, whose son was recently arrested charged with horse stealing and taken to Miles City. Berg has not been heard of since the raid and is believed to have fallen.[5]

In the face of such lawlessness—and without the benefit of any governmental agency for assistance—like the early settlers, the stock men turned to vigilantism. Perhaps they resorted to a tried-and-true heritage, or perhaps they felt they had no other choice, but vigilantism offered a means to control the growing threat to their property and livelihoods. Theft was a major topic of conversation during the 1884 Eastern Montana Stock Growers Convention in Miles City. The eastern Montana men, including Granville Stuart, weren't *publicly* enthusiastic about such proposals, a reticence that appeared to signal that they would take no action against such thefts. In hindsight, what Stuart wanted was absolute secrecy to carry out reprisals against thieves as far as they felt such actions warranted.

One newspaper article reported:

> *We learn from some of the cowboys who went with Con Kohrs' herd of cattle from the south fork of the Sun river to the new range beyond Maginnis, that horse thieves are very bad in that section of the country. Horses are night herded and in many cases kept under lock and key at night. A couple of Con Kohrs' horses were stolen, and several of Granville Stuart's.*[6]

A subset grouping of men met at the HDS ranch (the Hauser, Davis and Stuart Cattle Company) shortly after the Stock Growers Convention in May 1884. The men assembled were all brand holders, not hired hands. They likely regarded themselves as a vigilance committee and proceeded as such with two notable differences: instead of striking out immediately, they decided upon a course of caution—first, to wait one month, and second, to send out two members to gather more information on their targets. Another major difference was the degree of secrecy these men displayed. While there had always been an element of anonymity on the part of the vigilance committees, this time one senses that the men in charge knew that the times had changed. Judging from their lack of candor even years after the events took place, the men must have held concerns that history might judge them harshly.

Nevertheless, in their eyes the time had come to rein in lawlessness.

The fledgling settlement of Lewistown provided such an example of unprovoked violence when it erupted on the Fourth of July, 1884. Largely populated by Metis (of Indigenous and European ancestry), what happened at that town could have happened anywhere, but in this case the citizens had tired of such blights. While the newspaper provided a surprised accounting, it is recorded that Granville Stuart himself felt worried about the holiday celebration and warned ranchers that their livestock might be spirited away while they were in town celebrating. Stuart, along with many others in the region, knew—or assumed—that horse thieves and cattle rustlers were about. A particularly nasty pair of range thugs known as Rattlesnake Jack and Long-haired Owen (true names Charles Fallon and Charles Owen) had been seen locally.

Fallon and Owen had been drinking heavily when they spied a Metis named Bob Jackson dressed in an Uncle Sam costume at the horse races. He had worn that same costume during the earlier parade through Lewistown. Perhaps either Fallon or Owen had a horse that lost in the race, but words were exchanged and Owen, who held a grudge against Native tribes, pistol-whipped Jackson across the face, knocking him

Rip roaring fun. How the merchants and the cowboys of Butte City, Montana, run the local concert halls after their own fashion.
LIBRARY OF CONGRESS. 1886

down. When Jackson regained his footing and rose to standing, Owen forced him to lie face down on the ground again. Another Metis named Doney spoke up on behalf of Jackson and his poor treatment. The two range thugs eventually left to go into a saloon to drink even more, which, predictably, did nothing to improve their dispositions.

Now seriously drunk, the men emerged from the saloon and saw Doney. Long-haired Owen took aim at him and fired. He missed, as drunks tend to do. Doney shot back and hit Owen in the trigger finger. Owen switched gun hands and kept firing. The townspeople had had enough. The residents opened fire on both Fallon and Owen. One version of events portrayed Fallon, wounded and kneeling in the street alone, while Owen made his escape. In that version, Owen returned for his friend and found death by his side. Both men's bodies, in all accounts, were riddled with bullets.

An innocent bystander, a teenaged bullwhacker named Ben Smith, was also killed.

The bodies of Fallon and Owen were to be buried properly, but when a nearby resident complained, their "bodies were lassoed and dragged to a coulee out of town and buried with only some dirt thrown over them."[7]

Such events made many people want to rid Montana of the criminal element.

An article, written on July 24, 1884, sums up events to that point:

HORSE THIEVES

David Hilger and S. X. Swendeman, who arrived from Judith City yesterday, bring the startling information that five horse thieves were captured and hung in the vicinity of Rocky Point a few days ago. The word was brought to Judith just as they were taking their departure, and they did not get the particulars of the extraordinary event. The deed was done by a band of regularly organized cow boys, who set out to round up the thieves that infest that section, and they are doing their work in good shape. They secured thirty-two head of horses from the quintet of outlaws, and then made short work of them by hanging the lot to the nearest tree. . . . The stock men and other citizens are making it decidedly interesting for the outlaws that infest the region between the lower Judith and Musselshell. Within the past three weeks thirteen of them have been lynched, and it is probable the end is not yet. The campaign was opened up by the killing of two thieves on the Musselshell . . . two more were "fixed" in Lewiston on the Fourth, and the big haul at Rocky Point is the latest making in all thirteen victims. At this rate it will not take long to clean out the gang, and it is the only effective way to do it.[8]

At the time, there was a prevailing belief that a large, organized gang of horse thieves existed, numbering at least one hundred strong. The newspaper also, judging by its final words, approved of the vigilante actions.

Such happenings were quite possibly led by Granville Stuart, although others pursued similar goals. It was an open secret that Stuart had assumed the leadership of a group of men banded together who became known as "Stuart's Stranglers." A man who kept meticulous records, Stuart was certainly a prominent leader. And in his organization, he fostered or hired "Floppin' Bill" Cantrell, who acted as their point man. While Stuart campaigned for their cause, it was largely Cantrell who led the operations and logistics of the Horse Thief War.

One major shootout took place on the Missouri River. It came to be known as the Battle of Bates Point, after hostilities broke out between Stuart's "Stranglers" and eleven roughs led by a man known as "Stringer Jack."

On July 16, the vigilance committee, guided by a spy, "Floppin' Bill," who last winter visited this haunt and learned everything of interest pertaining thereto, arrived in sight. They surrounded it and found five men twenty yards south secreted in a tent, acting as watchmen. When the vigilance committee was discovered, a watchman preced[ed] toward the house to give notice. The signal gun was fired, and he fell dead. An action ensued, and two of the remaining inmates of the tent were killed, one wounded, and the other escaped unhurt. Sam Jones lived two hours after receiving his mortal wound and DISCLOSED THE INTRICACIES of their work. The vigilantes, exasperated by

View from center of town, Butte, Montana.

his story, proceeded to the house and demanded the surrender of the occupants, to which Jack Stringer the leader replied: "We will lick you sons of b—s." There were but eight vigilantes against eight criminals. The former, seeing the folly of attacking their fortifications, protected by loopholes, set fire to the stable, hoping it would reach the house and oust them. Unfavorable winds delayed its progress. A steamboat came in sight . . . and the vigilantes abandoned their plan of ejecting by fire as hopeless and hailed the boat for food. While they were gone the house was burned to the ground, the criminals escaping down the river in dugouts and only returning to bury their slain. The killed are Sam James, Sandy, and another man. Stringer Jack was wounded in the back, but escaped; Eugene Burr in an arm, and Dutchy in a foot. Five are here imprisoned, three killed, and five supposed to be eighteen miles below including Billy Donnes. At this house the vigilantes recovered thirty-five horses and twenty-nine at Donnes,' only a few miles distant.[9]

That same day, reportedly the vigilantes tracked Billy Downes (Donnes), an ex-wolfer, who had a dubious reputation and was well-known along the banks of the Missouri. There are conflicting accounts concerning this man's reputation, but it seems likely that he dealt in stolen goods. He was with another man named California Ed. Although the men protested that they had only stolen horses from tribes, there were twenty-six horses with well-known brands, and none of them their own. The vigilantes found a nearby grove of cottonwood trees and they strung the men up.

This act was not condoned by Stuart as Downes was a "family man" and the horses may have been of little value. That said, the valuation of horses bearing other outfit's brands were never figured into the equation of whether men lived or died.

Stories abound of cowhands riding out in the early morning hours and stumbling upon the work of the night riders.

Floppin' Bill Cantrell, the so-called spy mentioned above, was one of those Montana figures that loomed large. Even at the time, a lot was said about the man. Journalist W. W. Cheeley later wrote that there "wasn't a man in the entire country that could hold a candle to him in daring or recklessness. . . . [H]is name was feared . . . by every horse thief and out-law in central and northern Montana."[10] Another account claimed that "Floppin' Bill took the cake. He was . . . a perfect devil. . . . He would fight at the drop of a hat and drop that hat himself."[11]

In truth, "Floppin' Bill" was a stock inspector in the years 1884–1886, but that didn't mean that he shied away from a fight. The reputation of Cantrell as a hired killer worked well for the vigilantes, whether it was actually true or not.[12] Some accounts claimed that he had killed upward of thirty men, which seems unlikely but not impossible. The fact is that the number of men killed as horse thieves and cattle pirates will never be known.

The relatives of the murdered men did not stay silent, nor did all the citizens approve of such vigilante actions, no matter how the newspapers portrayed events. According to Teddy "Blue" Abbott, Granville Stuart's later son-in-law recounted, "There was a lot of bitterness in the country against Granville Stuart after the raids. But he never denied anything, nor did he tell who was with him. Once I heard a woman accuse him of hanging thirty innocent men. He raised his hat to her and said: 'Yes, madam, and by God, I done it alone.'"

There were also murmurings that Stuart had killed settlers to clear them off of rangeland that he wanted, but such murmurings have not been proven.[13]

Thankfully, the days of such extreme violence came to an end.

In 1885, House Bill (HB) 57, very similar to the failed HB 49, was presented. HB 57 allowed the governor to nominate and appoint a board of stock commissioners, with the legislature's upper house's assent. The board would consist of one member from each of the large stock-pro-ducing regions to make recommendations concerning the industry, and to deal with matters such as livestock theft through stock inspectors and detectives. Another beneficial feature provided for the appointment of a territorial veterinary surgeon who would investigate all cases of con-tagious or infectious diseases among livestock. The veterinarian would have the authority to order the slaughter of diseased animals, reporting directly to the governor. HB 57 did not seek to raise a mill levy on all properties but rather was assessed on the "valuation of all cattle, horses, mules and asses in their respective counties." There were exemptions for those small ranchers who owned less than eleven cows and three horses or three mules. This legislature session came to be known as the Cowboy Legislature, and HB 57 was signed into law on March 14, 1885.[14]

While rustling continued, this marks a shift into the modern era of range enforcement.

THE VIGILANTE CODE 3-7-77

The numbers 3-7-77 are recognized and attributed to the vigilantes. If the exact origins and meaning of the numbers are lost, the message they convey is one seemingly of menace. But Thomas Dimsdale, one contemporary of the vigilantes, makes no reference in his writings to any such code. Nathaniel Langford, likewise, makes no mention of those three numbers. In fact, while vigilantes pinned notes on their victims proclaiming their accused crimes (and thereby providing a measure of justification for the hangings)—that infamous code is never mentioned.

It seems unlikely that a definitive answer to the mystery will ever come to light.

There are three widely accepted theories (and possibly others) to explain the explicit meanings behind the now-famous sequence. One common theory is that 3-7-77 refers to the dimensions of a grave. Three feet wide, seven feet long, and seventy-seven inches deep. Another theory relates to the amount of time a miscreant was afforded to leave the territory: three hours, seven minutes, and seventy-seven seconds. Who would have been timing departures is another question up for debate.

Then there is the next option: the fact that 3-7-77 came from either California or Colorado, signifying vigilante member numbers: member number three, member number seven, and member number seventy-seven signified, in some theories, that individual mason number three, seven, and seventy-seven could authorize burials and execution. Additionally, Colorado's vigilante organization claimed seventy-seven members at its inception, that's as far as that theory goes. In neither Colorado nor California is that numeric sequence or code widely recognized.

Code 3-7-77 is likely a Montana invention.

Montana Supreme Court Justice Lew Callaway entered into the fray with an article he wrote in 1929. Callaway, a mason, refuted the possibility that the code had masonic associations or ties. He insisted that Colorado and California vigilantes used two codes, 3-7-77 and 3-11-77.[15] But as stated earlier, neither of those two states recognize the sequence, other than in relation to Montana. N. P. Langford, on the other hand, ties the masons together with 3-7-77. Langford's source or basis comes from a death. On November 12, 1862, William H. Bell, a mason, died of Mountain Fever in Bannack. Before his death, he asked for a masonic funeral—a request made to Nathaniel Langford himself.

Robert Miller, a chronicler of the mason's first hundred years in Montana, and citing Callaway, claims that eleven of the first twelve vigilantes in Montana were masons. Miller also claims that seventy-six masons attended William Bell's funeral—so adding the deceased to that number provides the number of seventy-seven masons present. Miller studied the numerology important to the masons: it required three to make a lodge, seven to make it perfect, and again, seventy-seven masons were called to this first meeting in Bannack, which was Bell's funeral.

Rex Myers, in his article, mentions a thesis written by William Trimble in 1914 stating matter-of-factly, "that notice of a meeting was given by posting 3-7-77."[16]

Thus, while the mystery continues, the uneasiness of the vague threat signified by 3-7-77 hangs in the air.

CHAPTER 13

THE DEVIL'S PERCH, BLACK HEART OF, AND OTHER NAMES

BUTTE (THE GOLDEN AGE OF UNIONISM)

The devil's perch. In some ways, maybe people were just jealous when they used names like these to describe Butte, the mining capital of Montana. A workhorse of a city, Butte proved strong, vibrant, and wealthy. In fact, Butte didn't take much guff—especially from locales that deemed themselves more *refined*. Refinement—in the mining sense of the word—was a major obstacle to overcome, but overcome it they did. And that victory paved the way for the riches that flowed in (or rather were extracted) and allowed those fabulous fortunes to become obtainable.

Butte's famous hill was first noticed in the spring of 1856 when Caleb Irvine and a trading party camped along what would become Dublin Gulch. There they found a trench dug in quartz using elk antlers—but who did the initial digging remains unknown. This discovery would later become known as the Original Lode.[1] In the warm months of 1864, prospectors moved into the region of Butte and worked the placers. By 1867 there were approximately two thousand miners in the region, working along the banks of the Silver Bow Creek. The settlements, camps, and the like were referred to collectively as the Silver Box Camps in those early days. Butte's population at this point was estimated at three hundred to five hundred people—predominantly male, rough and ramshackle in appearance. That rough and ramshackle appearance could be applied to the miners, the buildings, and the camp they constructed. Early observers labeled Butte as "deplorable" and filled to the brim with the inevitable "hurdy-gurdy houses and 'wide-open' gambling dens."[2] By 1868, early Butte fell into decline, and with the drought of 1869, so did the Silver Bow Camps.

Nevertheless, as gold production declined and the placers played out, a determined group of four men constructed a crude blast furnace in the attempt to smelt the black quartz reefs that held manganese and silver. Joseph Ramsdell, Billy Parks, Dennis Leary, and Charles Porter sent tons of the matte (the initial product after smelting copper sulfide ore) away to either St. Louis or, remarkably, to Swansea, Wales, for further smelting.[3] The experiment was considered unsuccessful, although the source of this matte would later become known as the Parrot Lode. At the time, no one had either the technology nor the transportation facilities to make the matte pay, with railheads hundreds of miles away. Butte dwindled further and almost died.

But, as everyone knows, the story of Butte didn't die there.

The 1870s and the 1873 Panic caused by bank failures didn't do the district many favors. Control of mines slipped away from individuals as they were bought up by capitalists (or merchant-financiers) who bought cheaply and had the deep pockets necessary for capital investment. The likes of A. J. Davis and Samuel T. Hauser found prospects in the Silver Bow district attractive and formed a partnership. Davis started buying up properties, and the banker Samuel Hauser helped finance the ventures. Davis became Butte's first millionaire. Then came the more famous William Andrews Clark in 1872. Much is written of Clark and his business genius and all-consuming ambition. Irish immigrant Marcus Daly arrived as well and is still regarded as one of the greatest practical miners and developers ever known. Whereas Clark was viewed as taciturn, and Daly as possessing an abundance of charm, it stands to reason that the two men did not throw in together, but instead became rivals for the fortunes of Butte.

A frontier post office, eastern Montana. Photograph shows individuals, some on horseback and others riding in wagons, waiting outside of a post office.
LIBRARY OF CONGRESS. CA. 1880–1890

On December 26, 1881, the much-needed and long-awaited railroad reached Butte. However, in 1882, a gentleman's agreement between the Utah and Northern spur of the Union Pacific and the Northern Pacific railroads divided up the territories. This agreement still meant high freight rates for Butte ores, dampening prospects for a time.

The Anaconda mine, located by Michael Hickey, was an average silver prospect in those days. Together with his brother Edward, the Hickeys located many claims in the area. A large quartz boom struck after 1876, and several men with deeper pockets than the Hickeys showed an interest in purchasing the Anaconda. Marcus Daly worked out a purchase agreement with Michael Hickey and his partner, Charles X. Larabie, whereby he purchased the Anaconda for a mere $30,000—Larabie received $20,000 and Hickey $10,000 for his one-third ownership. This was in the autumn of 1880, and Daly needed backers. He attracted George Hurst, James Ben Ali Haggin, and Lloyd Tevis for financial partnership.[4]

Copper began to edge out silver—the Silver Repeal of 1894 made it clear that copper was now king, and Butte stood in an excellent position to take advantage of its riches. And riches poured from the ground to the tune of "210,000,000 pounds of copper a year . . . and employing 8,000 men with a payroll equivalent to $44,000,000 a month in today's dollars. . . . The by-product gold and silver amounted to some $500,000,000 a year, again at present-day value."[5]

But this is not an account of the so-called copper kings, but rather the story of a town and the average people who lived in an affluent yet polluted environment. Arsenic-laced smoke killed every tree and every blade of grass in town. Sulfur smelter-smoke equated to the more picturesque name of brimstone—a noxious combination that smelt like hell. In addition to these industrial poisons released into the air, Butte utilized five slaughterhouses that disposed of gory remnants along the edge of town, and open sewers rounded out the notes of Butte's fragrance.

While the wealthy might have lived like royalty, at least they enjoyed the same aroma as the working man.

Not surprisingly, for all the wealth coming out of the ground, there were segments in society where affluence did not reach beyond their simple wages, and life could remain downright hard, dangerous, and deadly. The backbone of Butte remained mining, pure and simple. And to pull those riches out of the earth required miners. And mining is, and was, a dangerous profession riddled by accidents, lung illnesses, and uncertainty. Miners are stereotyped for their hardworking and hard-drinking ways. No doubt the accompanying cast of characters certainly made their presence known in Butte: the gamblers, the saloon keepers, and most certainly the prostitutes. Butte boasted, and fostered, a wide-open town that offered no apologies as emigrants from all over the world poured into her mines and streets, contributing to the multicultural and multifaceted location it remains today. While the majority of Butte's miners were single men, Butte transformed into a family town, unlike the earliest mining camps. While the single miners sought entertainment and lived in boarding houses, churches, schools, and a library offered a different type of consolation and added a stabilizing influence into the raucous mix.

The large boarding houses often had poor sanitary conditions, which led to increased incidents of disease. All of this was above ground. Fatalities of one stripe or another stalked the underground workers relentlessly. As a result, Butte became a stronghold of unionization in response to working conditions and safety issues. Measures to address the environment were decades away in the future.

"It used to kill them pretty lively then."[6] So went the testimony of deputy mine inspector Frank Hunter in 1897, referring to the dangerous hanging wall in the St. Lawrence Mine where he had worked in 1890. As one author phrased it,

> *During its heyday, the late nineteenth and early twentieth centuries, Butte was indeed a quintessential mining town. An air of transience, fatalism, and ribaldry, so typical of western mining camps, pervaded the place. Long after impressive business blocks rose up to symbolize its urbanity, Butte continued to consider itself a "camp," like a suddenly rich wastrel who could not fathom her riches. Butte was self-conscious of its ugliness, its cultural isolation, of its wild side. Above all, Butte was frenetic.*[7]

The cause of it all remained mining, until the bottom fell out at the end of World War I.

Reading a two months' sample of any newspaper at the time portrays the frenetic past that Butte was famous for.

January 1899

Jan. 3—G. H. Casey sues to recover thirteen pieces of ground, embraced in the surface of the Thomas lode.

Jan. 6—Mike Pino and Tim Bilboa killed in Never Sweat Mine.

Jan. 6—James Ryan, assaulted in a Butte saloon a week before, dies at hospital from the wounds.

Jan. 12—Thomas Smith and Peter Sullivan killed at Mountain Con. Mine.

Jan. 14—Joe Melvich and Joe Maxwell killed at the Colusa-Parrot.

Jan. 14—Tim McGuin and Louis Herstad badly injured in Anaconda mine.

Jan. 25—Anaconda Hibernians decide to aid Boers with men and money.

Jan. 30—F. V. Browne killed at the Mountain Con. Mine.

Jan. 30—F. A. Heinze wins suit involving the Michael Davitt Lode.

Jan. 30—W. R. Conn acquitted in Anaconda of the murder of Woolford.

February 1899

Feb. 15—Fred Huber injured in accident at the Diamond Mine.

Feb. 15—Ed. T. Colby stabbed by H. W. Peters on West Park Street.

Feb. 17—Big strike reported in the Parrot.

Feb. 18—Early closing movement endorsed at mass meeting.

Feb. 19—Charles Allen stabbed by W. A. Strasser.

Feb. 21—Joseph Gannon shot and killed by John Kehoe in a Butte saloon, in self-defense.

Feb. 22—Henry Jeffries killed in the Moose Mine.

Feb. 23—Milton Keller crushed in the Moonlight Mine.

Feb. 23—Blanche Stone commits suicide.

Feb. 23—E. R. Chase found dead in his room on East Park Street.[8]

Some mines in Butte gained the reputation of particularly dangerous places to work, for fatal reasons.

After the gold placers ran out and copper became king, the first miners were often of Irish, Cornish, or German origin. These miners had experience, and the Cornish and German miners had usually completed long apprenticeships. Starting above ground sorting ores when between nine and twelve years old, the youth gradually were sent underground with relatives to teach them the trade. Most times they began as muckers (shoveling ore into carts) and would have grown into more technical duties underground as they completed the stages of their training. Obviously, those underground tasks became more technical and dangerous as the miners progressed. There was much to recommend this method. Mining, like blacksmithing or carpentry, required skill and training. The lack thereof showed up in accidents and fatalities. Also of benefit was a commonality of the English language shared between the Americans, Cornish, and Irish. Directions, explanations, and warnings were commonly understood when given. In the early days of Butte mining, light was provided by candles and ore carts were hauled through the mines by mules, donkeys, or horses. Surprisingly enough, the "old-fashioned" mining ways of the 1860s and 1870s proved safer to the men than the advances in technology that arrived in the 1880s and 1890s. Of course, the mining companies welcomed the new inventions. They saw productivity rise from a yearly 20,000 pounds of copper mined per man in 1887 to 32,000 yearly pounds of copper in 1896.[9]

And while the profits were tallied, the listings in the obituaries increased.

Machine drills replaced the handheld wedges and sledges. Improvements in hoisting and tramming added an element of speed hitherto unknown. The old tramming and hoisting of the 1870s and earlier consisted of horse or mule drawn ore carts in the instance of tramming (transporting ore from the stopes [tunnels or shafts] to the level station). That slow, steady progression was replaced by locomotives. Even more worrisome were the hoisting mechanisms. Once, the cages used to be pulled up by horses winding steel rope on a winch in a slow process. When steam or electrically powered engines replaced the horse whims and windlasses, both men and ore could ascend and descend with dazzling speed. While all methods had their own particular hazards, speed proved deadly. In 1887, cage-related deaths comprised 33 percent of the fatalities. That number rose to 35 percent in 1896. By 1889, Montana required the use of iron-bonneted cages and safety gates to protect the miners from falling rock overhead, and from physically falling out from the cages themselves. Men lost their lives when hoist engineers became distracted and missed the stops, sending the cages into the sheaves of the head frames above. Also, ropes could snap, sending the cages careening downward toward certain death. Safety dogs (safety equipment catches/ breaks) could fail—and did. And while mining by open-flamed candle might sound dangerous, the introduction of electricity into the mines created a new set of hazards. Carelessly suspended trolley wire carried electrical current that could collide with the carbide lamps attached to the miner's hat, causing inevitable electrocution. While the trolley wire was usually housed in wooden troughs, contact could still occur. Unfortunately, many of these dangers became more pronounced with the introduction of unskilled miners into the underground operations— oftentimes miners who did not speak English enough to reliably give or understand warnings and cautions. These cultural differences between the English speakers and the newly arrived immigrants played out not just below ground but in the streets and homes of Butte above.

Butte was a melting pot of ethnicities, giving it the most diverse population in the state of Montana. In the early days of Butte, the populace was predominately single male miners and purveyors, along with the sporting women and the occasional wives and daughters of the merchants and mine bosses. During this time, the primary language spoken remained English in various dialects and accents. By 1880 and the arrival of the railroad, the makeup of Butte started to change. The ranks of the existing Cornish, Irish, and Americans swelled with the arrivals of Germans, French Canadians, and the Scandinavians: Norwegians, Swedes, and the industrious Finns. Also present were British Canadians, Jews, and Christian Lebanese peddlers and merchants. Native Americans were represented—Cree, Chippewa, and Metis (mixed blood)—and the Chinese had a distinct presence as well. Before long (in the 1890s), the Italians arrived, as did desperately poor people from the Slavic countries. These last two groups were often referred to as "dark men" and animosity between the fairer-skinned early arrivals and these newer groups boiled over. In the end, however, Butte eventually assimilated all comers, to weave one of the state's richest tapestries.

But life did not prove easy, and economic, racial, religious, and political tensions rose and frayed. Most of these groups settled in specific neighborhoods or enclaves, and they built their own churches and halls, saloons, and communities. Long-held beliefs from the Old World could spill over into the new, with the Cornish holding on to their Methodist persuasions, the Irish practicing Catholicism, the Serbs and Croatians adhering to Eastern Orthodoxy, and so on. The Finns were interesting and found great favor with Copper King Marcus Daly because of their strength and athleticism. Interestingly, the Finnish immigrants were also staunch socialists, supporting and acting as leaders of the labor movements. Which, unsurprisingly, went against the Copper Kings and their insatiable desire for wealth. The Chinese created a Chinatown and suffered from white prejudice. The district's first hanging was that of a Chinaman, strung up by two whites for no identifiable reason at all. Like other Montana locales, vigilantism reared its head at the relatively advanced year of 1881, but in Butte the committee limited itself to written warnings. As a point of differentiation, no Butte hangings in the name of vigilantism were committed.

The economics of the varied ethnic groups came into play in Butte, as they likely did in every city across America. Butte made no pretenses about where its money came from. The downtown district was centrally located, with the residences of the wealthy located on the western side. To the south and southwest, workmen built in brick or constructed wooden framed houses that stretched down toward the "flats" and the railroad tracks—never the best of locales. The noted slum of Butte, the Cabbage Patch, was a six-block area characterized by poverty, vice, and violence located in the southeast portion of the city. To the north and the east of the city mines proliferated. More mines along with more mines. Tunnels crisscrossed underneath the whole city; there were possibly 10,000 miles of such tunnels.

In fact, the Berkeley Pit consumed a couple of colorful neighborhoods in its widening yaw: Dublin Gulch and Meaderville. Dublin Gulch originally housed the Irish and later the Slavs, and Meaderville became first an Italian stronghold, later turning into a Slavic one. In time, the Berkeley Pit would consume or threaten more ethnic neighborhoods, including Finn Town. Each district, enclave, or neighborhood had its own characteristics. The west side of Butte where the Copper Kings built their elaborate mansions seemed a world away from Chinatown, located within a stone's throw of the red-light district.

What went on both above ground and below was reflected in Butte's underworld and red-light districts.

> Vulgar manner, overfed,
> Overdressed and underbred.
> Heathen godless—hell's delight.
> Nude by day and lewd by night.
> Dwarfed the man, enlarged the brute.
> Ruled by roué and prostitute.
> Purple robed and pauper clad.
> Raving, rotting, money-mad.
> Squirming herd in Mammon's mesh,
> Wilderness of human flesh.
> Crazed by Avarice, Lust and Rum.
> Butte, thy name is Delirium.[10]

The above poem provides a contemporaneous look into the seedier side of Butte at the turn of the last century.

No matter what source is consulted, the most prevalent description of Butte was "wide-open." That wide openness was not entirely what set Butte apart from the rest of the state, but rather it was its wild side. By 1893 the city directory listed 212 "drinking establishments," sporting such names as the Bucket of Blood and the Clipper Shades. Many of Butte's bars were open twenty-four hours a day and never closed.

Gambling was also a popular pastime, and there were sixteen licensed gambling "hells." Prostitution, however, reportedly "came to rank as one of Butte's livelihoods."[11] In the 1870s, the red-light district was located along the central business district on Park Street. In time, it moved to Galena Street, and in the 1890s, the parlor houses on Mercury Street reigned supreme. The Dumas was the jewel in the crown, and Irish World a close contender. Across the street were cribs, and cribs lined the alley behind the Dumas. Interestingly enough, on the Sanborn Fire Maps of Butte in 1890, the alley is listed as "unpassable." The owners of the buildings were not always the people who ran them: instead, notable figures held the land as investment properties. Helena millionaire Anton Holter owned the Blue Range in 1897, and Butte newspaper magnate and former US Senator Lee Mantle purchased the holding from him in 1900. The Dumas was built and maintained by French-Canadian brothers Joseph and Arthur Nadaeu, who registered the building under the name of Joseph's wife, Delia. Remarkably, Delia made her way into Butte's "high society" with everyone quite clear as to the source of the family's wealth. In time, Arthur returned to Montreal, but Joseph remained in Butte to manage the family's investments. The Nadeaus, early residents of Butte, were listed in the 1880 census as a family . . . along with gamblers and saloonkeepers who resided with them. In those years, the Nadeaus made their money from running a hotel and restaurant on west Broadway. In time, they sold that business and by 1895 Joseph was listed as a "capitalist" in the city directory. The Dumas, built by the Nadeaus in 1890, reflected much of Butte itself. Originally, the first floor contained lavish ballrooms and banquet rooms, while the bedrooms upstairs were for the women who were most in demand. These areas were frequented by the elite of Butte who had no need to ask the price of whatever commodities they desired. Downstairs, however, a different world churned. The Dumas's basement held a myriad of subterranean cribs that were leased by "less desirable" women, and whose customers were predominantly working-class miners.

THE CHINESE IN BUTTE AND PROSTITUTION

Violence in the Chinese community remained a threat, as it was in all places of prostitution. The following rather unkind account illustrates a couple of important points. First, that the woman called You Kim had reportedly been "purchased" and was unable to dictate her future. She suffered as a result. It is also interesting to note that the perpetrator had a connection to the mayor of Butte for whom he worked as a servant, as well as functioning as an apparent procurer. This unfortunate woman obviously felt that the traditional Chinese methods of law enforcement would not provide any measure of protection, and so took her chances by turning to the American justice system.

Bathed in Her Gore
You Kim Hatcheted in the Back
Bloody Tragedy in China Town

At twenty minutes to three o'clock yesterday afternoon a bleeding Chinese woman rushed into the Police court, supported on either side by a fellow Mongolian, and after a five minutes' torrent of gibberish gave the Court to understand that she had been chopped in the back with a hatchet by one Gong Sing, her former owner. Gong Sing had sold her for $1,200 to another almond-eyed Celestial, and instead of delivering the goods, demanded more money. When this was refused, he seized a hatchet, and as the fair You Kim sat in front of him, chopped her deliberately in the back about one inch to the right of the spine, at about the point where President Garfield was shot. The blow cut through clothing and all, and with a little more force would doubtless have inflicted a mortal wound. A warrant for assault with intent to commit murder was instantly issued, and Gong Sing was soon languishing in prison. He will have a preliminary examination this morning. Soon after his arrest he sent for Mayor Beal, with whom he has worked for some three years as a valued servant. For such a deadly offense high bail was required, and Gong Sing [spent] last night behind bars.[12]

Not all the Chinese in Butte were involved at the lowest rungs of society. Dr. Huie Pock, an herbal doctor in Butte, made his fortune practicing traditional Chinese medicine, along with acupuncture. Dr. Pock treated Chinese, Chinese American, and European American patients. Dr. Pock's practice moved into prominence when he successfully treated the ulcers of a daughter of William Andrews Clark—a Copper King and one of the wealthiest men in America. On a less salubrious note, it is alleged that he also assisted prostitutes with remedies for sexually transmitted diseases and herbs to induce miscarriages.[13]

Life in the cribs could be brutal. Violence accompanied the prostitution trade, and those women without protection in the cribs made obvious targets. By 1910 as the age of the Copper Kings faded, the red-light district declined along with the fortunes of the town. The wealthy patrons returned East, and the high-dollar banquets and lavish entertainment were no longer in fashion. The Dumas divided the former ball and reception rooms into bedrooms on the first floor as a sign of the changing environment and time. The girls who inhabited those rooms might not have been the queens of the row, but they were considered above those who plied their trade out of the basement cribs or even worse, in the shacks of Venus Alley.

Prostitution in the town would linger until 1982, when the Dumas Brothel finally closed.

LABOR UNIONS

The first miner's union formed in 1878 in the silver-producing years; it was known as the Butte Workingmen's Union. This general union allowed all workers, regardless of craft, and grew to an estimated 1,800 dues-paying members by 1885. In that same year, it reorganized as the Butte Miner's Union. In a break with its previous membership, it became a union for miners exclusively and the other trades were spun off into their own formations, creating thirty-four separate unions that represented nearly all six thousand workers. Established as one of the most solidly union cities in the country, union dues–paying membership prevailed in all industries. One major accomplishment of the Miner's Union was the "closed shop" agreement with the mining companies—meaning that the companies would hire only union workers. In May 1893, the Butte Miner's Union transformed into the Western Federation of Miners and took pride of place as it became Local Number One.

This golden era for unions held until 1899, the year that ushered in the age of copper company consolidations. Remarkably at that time, this trend toward consolidations was accompanied by a dire warning from Governor R. B. Smith, a Populist-Democrat with ties to Daly: "If you do not assert your independence now and defeat this measure, it will be too late when the tentacles of this octopus have fastened their fangs on the strong limbs of this fair commonwealth."[14] While the analogy might come across as mixed and garbled, the lawmakers ignored his warning and the Amalgamated Copper Mining Company was born. Backed by Daly, it was a "holding company," which, like others of the time, were designed to own and control the actual operating companies, thus enacting consolidations. James Ben Ali Haggin cashed in his Anaconda holdings after participating in forming the Amalgamated. Daly stayed on as president. He was more of a figurehead, with Henry Rogers acting as vice president and William G. Rockefeller as secretary/treasurer. The directors of the trust included those men, plus other Wall Street notables. This marked the point in time when "control of Butte and its destiny now rested in Wall Street hands."[15] In 1915 the outcome remained unknown, but this entity would become the powerful Anaconda Copper Mining Company. The battle lines were drawn, pitting the workingmen and labor unions against the powerful interests of Wall Street and Standard Oil.

A period of blood, labor unrest, "rustling cards," and blacklists began, culminating in a stark mining disaster with 168 fatalities, and a 3-7-77 lynching of Industrial Workers of the World (IWW) Frank Little in 1917. Butte's eventual decline was written "in the cards"; Butte would prove resilient to challenges, but her heyday waned.

CHAPTER 14

RARE HISTORY

Montana's history is evident everywhere, on every road, gulch, rolling hill, mountainside, and mine tailing. It's written on the old, weathered boards of the ghost towns and on the cross beams of ranch roads, and it lurks in the corners of old saloons. Everywhere a person

Montana woman in cowgirl attire on horseback.
LIBRARY OF CONGRESS. CA. 1909

can turn, if they look beneath the surface, they can find the traces of old Montana and the fight against man and elements to carve out a life in the state. Not all the actions were good or fair, but they all contributed to the tapestry of the State of Montana as it is today.

As time moves forward, perhaps more histories will become known and better understood. There are still many discoveries left to be made.

APPENDIX A

US Military Installations in Montana Territory

Uniquely characteristic of Montana is the manner in which fur-trapping posts, trading posts, military outposts, and forts often flowed from one use into another. This fluid nature meant that often a location called a "fort" might have actually been a trading post. This section is intended to highlight US military installations/forts/structures. Other "forts" may be listed in the fur trapping section.

Fort Assinniboine—Established May 9, 1879, seven miles south of Havre. It was abandoned in 1911. This was the largest of Montana's military installations, built to prevent Sitting Bull's re-entry into the area from Canada. At the fort's peak, it had 104 buildings constructed mainly from local red brick for a complement of 36 officers and 453 noncommissioned officers and enlisted men. The structures were built in the frontier style to optimize cavalry operations. First Lieutenant John Pershing served at the fort beginning in 1896 and was attached to the 10th US Cavalry.[1]

Fort Belknap—Despite the late date, this fort was established for the North West Company as a fur trading post in 1871. This nonmilitary post was discontinued in 1886 and is now located on the Fort Belknap Indian Reservation, which was established in 1888.[2]

Fort Benton—This outpost began as a fur trading post in 1848. Started by Alexander Culbertson for the American Fur company, it was later sold to Northwest Fur in 1865. After a continued decline in the fur trade, the post was sold to the military in 1868. First garrisoned in October 11, 1869, the fort was abandoned May 31, 1881.[3]

Fort Cooke—Established in 1866, Fort Cooke was located at the mouth of the Judith River on the Missouri River. Built to protect the steamboat trade by the Thirteenth Infantry Regiment, it was demolished in April 1870. This fort was often called Camp Cooke, and confusion with a Fort Claggett nearby is common. Fort Claggett was a trading post established to provide supplies to soldiers and was not a US military installation.[4]

Fort Custer—Constructed in 1877 and decommissioned in 1898 in Hardin, Montana. In 1892 the fort housed many "buffalo soldiers" (term used by Native tribes for African American troops).[5]

Fort Elizabeth Meagher—Built in May 1867 in response to Sioux and Crow hostilities and the death of John Bozeman in April 1867. Located on the Bridger Pass approaches, the fort was active until Fort Ellis was established at the end of August.[6]

Fort Ellis—Established August 27, 1867, it was active until August 2, 1886 (decommissioned). This fort was very active in the Indian Wars: the Marias's Massacre, the Great Sioux War (1867–1877), and the Nez Perce War (1877).[7]

Fort Keogh—Built in 1876 at the western edge of what is now Miles City, this fort came on the heels of the resounding defeat at the Little Bighorn, and its initial purpose was to prevent the Cheyenne and Sioux from escaping into Canada. Originally called "The Cantonment on Tongue River," it was first scouted out in 1873 by Colonel David S. Stanley who thought it would be a good location for a military supply hub. The Cantonment's name changed to Fort Keogh on November 8, 1878, to commemorate Myles Keogh who fell at the Little Bighorn. The fort was active until 1924. Of interesting note: This fort processed more horses for World War I than any other fort.[8]

Fort Logan—Established on November 1, 1869, in Meagher County, this military post was established to protect the gold-mining camps and the Fort Benton trade route. Originally named Camp Baker, the name was changed in 1877 in memory of Captain Logan, who had served at the fort and was killed at the Big Hole Battle engagement with Chief Joseph. It was active until 1880.[9]

Fort Maginnis—The last of five forts built after Custer's defeat at the Little Bighorn, the fort was abandoned July 20, 1890, at what was deemed the end of the Indian Wars, and its buildings were sold to the public. It was a large installation.[10]

Fort Missoula—"Established as a permanent military post in 1877 and built in response to requests of local townspeople and settlers for protection in the event of conflict with western Montana tribes. It was intended as a major outpost for the region; however, area residents also were quite aware of the payroll, contracts, and employment opportunities Fort Missoula would provide. Fort Missoula . . . was an 'open fort,' a design common for posts located west of the Mississippi, except during its time used as an Alien Detention Center during WWII."[11] It was decommissioned in April 2001.

Fort Parker—Built in 1869, this was a functioning fort nine miles from Livingston, but in 1875 it was moved near Absarokee on the Stillwater River. This was the first Crow Indian Agency and has a dark history with the Crow people. "There are mixed emotions when discussing Fort Parker," shared George Reed, Crow Cultural Committee chairman. "Somewhere between Fort Parker and Livingston is the place, Bisshiilan-nuusaao, where the Apsáalooke placed the government issued rations and the khaki army blankets on the ground and burned them; somehow they found out they were festered with the small pox germ."[12]

Fort Shaw—Established in 1867 to protect the road from Fort Benton to Helena. During the 1876 campaign against the Sioux and Cheyenne, Colonel John Gibbon, the base commander, led the garrison up the Missouri River; procured reinforcements at Fort Ellis, Montana; rendezvoused with the forces of General Alfred Terry on the Yellowstone at the mouth of the Rosebud; and subsequently relieved the survivors of Custer's regiment at the Little Bighorn. The following year, troops from Forts Shaw, Ellis, and Missoula, again under Gibbon, defeated the nontreaty Nez Perce, retreating from Idaho to Montana at the Battle of the Big Hole.

After the Army relinquished the fort in 1891, the Department of the Interior used it as a tribal school for many years.[13]

Fort C. F. Smith—Opened August 12, 1866, during Red Cloud's War. Established by order of Col. Henry B. Carrington, it was one of five forts proposed to protect the Bozeman Trail against the Oglala Lakota tribe—a violation of the 1851 Treaty of Fort Laramie. The fort was abandoned in 1868 and burned by the Sioux under Red Cloud in 1868 under the Second Treaty of Fort Laramie. This was the location of the Hayfield Fight in 1867, when warriors unsuccessfully attacked a party of twenty hay cutters.[14]

APPENDIX B

MEN WHO SURVIVED THE LITTLE BIGHORN BUT DIED WITHIN TEN YEARS

The following list has been gleaned from the Seventh US Cavalry Roster 1876. Additional information has been linked.

James Akers—August 3, 1881, in Nez Perce battle at Canyon Creek. Cause of death phthisis pulmonalis (tuberculosis). He was thirty years of age at death. Sgt James Akers (1851–1881) – Find a Grave Memorial

Abram B. Brant—October 4, 1878. Killed by accidental gunshot wound to the stomach when handing over gun to sergeant the day before he was to be awarded the Medal of Honor for bringing water to the wounded under extremely dangerous circumstances. https://valor.militarytimes .com/hero/32.

Alexander Brown—April 7, 1884. From Scotland. Battle of the Washita, Battle of the Little Big Horn, Battle of Canyon Creek. Problem with alcohol, had tertiary syphilis. Discharged on disability with partial paralysis. Cause of death locomotor atax (inability to coordinate muscular movements per Find a Grave). https://www.menwithcuster.com/05/ ?doing_wp_cron=1665702151.8685190677642822265625

Jeremiah Campbell—May 8,1884. Deaf in right ear and struck by rail car he failed to hear approach. https://littlebighorn.info/Cavalry/NameC .htm#JeremiahCampbell.

Patrick Coakley—November 13, 1881. Soldier's Home, Washington, D.C. Detached Service when the battle occurred. Cause of death gastritis from intemperance and hemostasis. https://www.menwithcuster.com/ in-the news/?doing_wp_cron=1665703078.4441270828247070312500.

David Cooney—July 21, 1876. Fort Abraham Lincoln. Shot in the hip at the battle, died later of "an infection of the bloodstream." Sgt. David Cooney (1848–1876) – Find a Grave Memorial.

Michael Crowe—June 8, 1883. Fort Yates. Cause of death heart disease. https://littlebighorn.info/Cavalry/NameC.htm#JeremiahCampbell.

Michael Delaney—February 12, 1884. On Detached Service. No other information located. Michael Delaney (1854–1884) – Find a Grave Memorial.

Milton Delacy—September 2, 1885. No other information located. Seventh Cavalry – Surnames Beginning with D (littlebighorn.info).

Alexander Downing—August 2, 1884 (was on Detached Service). No other information located. Seventh Cavalry – Surnames Beginning with D (littlebighorn.info).

Edwin Eckerson—August 17,1885. En route to join the battle. No further details on cause of death. https://www.littlebighorn.info/Cavalry/NameE.htm#EdwinEckerson.

Hugo Findeisen—May 21, 1881 (on Detached Service when battle occurred). Suicide while in the fort hospital; cut his throat with a blade. https://www.littlebighorn.info/Cavalry/NameF.htm.

Samuel Foster—May 26, 1884. No other information located. Seventh Cavalry – Surnames Beginning with F (littlebighorn.info).

William Frank—April 6, 1880. No other information located. Seventh Cavalry – Surnames Beginning with F (littlebighorn.info).

Andrew Fredericks—January 14, 1881. Fort Totten D. T. Cause of death Pyaemia—blood poisoning (septicemia) caused by the spread in the bloodstream of pus-forming bacteria released from an abscess. Sgt. Andrew Fredericks (1844–1881) – Find a Grave Memorial.

Thomas French—March 27, 1882. Commanded Company M. Court-martialed on January 13, 1879, for being drunk on duty. Sentence commuted. Cause of death listed as apoplexy. Note service record: Civil War Veteran (wounded), Battle of Little Big Horn, Battle of Canyon Creek Nez Perce War, kicked in the head by a horse and suffered trauma 1878. https://gloverparkhistory.com/civil-war/local-people-in-the-civil-war/thomas-henry-french/.

Peter Gannon—June 12, 1886. Detached service during the Little Bighorn. Enlisted four times but deserted once. Died of localized chronic peritonitis. Washita campaign prior to Little Bighorn. https://www.menwithcuster.com/18/.

William Montell George—July 3, 1876. Succumbed to battle wounds on the *Far West* steamer.

William M. Harris—June 9, 1885. Medal of Honor. Cause of death unknown. William M Harris (1851–1885) – Find a Grave Memorial.

George Heid—February 1, 1877. No further information. Seventh Cavalry – Surnames Beginning with H (littlebighorn.info).

Frederick Holmstead—March 27, 1880. Fort Abraham Lincoln. Consumption. Frederick Holmstead (littlebighorn.info).

Charles H. Houghtaling—August 14, 1881. Fort Lewis, Colorado. Acute bronchitis. Pvt. Charles H. Houghtaling (unknown-1881) – Find a Grave Memorial.

Charles Kavanaugh—February 14, 1886. Died in the National Soldiers' Home, Washington, D.C. Most veterans who entered the Soldiers' Home suffered from a host of physical and psychological maladies that developed as a result of their military service. Seventh Cavalry – Surnames Beginning with K (littlebighorn.info).

George H. King—July 2, 1876, Location of death given as Pease Bottom, Montana. Died on the *Far West* steamer. Corp. George H. King (1848–1876) – Find a Grave Memorial.

James Lawler—September 18, 1877. Canyon Creek Montana Territory. Detached Service during the Little Bighorn. Died in Nez Perce battle. Seventh Cavalry – Surnames Beginning with L (littlebighorn.info).

William Logue—deemed insane at one point, he remained in the army until 1884, when he was accidentally shot in the toe. https://billingsgazette.com/news/features/magazine/haunted-by-history-tragedy-followed-bighorn-battle-survivors/article_a5fd2a85-616e-5aeb-a183-449ce45a0410.html.

Daniel Mahoney—1885 at thirty-three years old. Died of exhaustion at the Soldiers' Home. https://billingsgazette.com/news/features/magazine/haunted-by-history-tragedy-followed-bighorn-battle-survivors/article_a5fd2a85-616e-5aeb-a183-449ce45a0410.html.

Thomas F. McLaughlin—1886. North Dakota Hospital of the Insane. https://billingsgazette.com/news/features/magazine/haunted-by-history-tragedy-followed-bighorn-battle-survivors/article_a5fd2a85-616e-5aeb-a183-449ce45a0410.html.

Michael P. Madden—December 18, 1883. Leg amputated. Died of (likely) alcoholism. Buried in Potter's Field. Michael Madden (littlebighorn.info). Additional sources: (1) "An Agreeable Sort When Sober": the Myth of Michael Madden: Additions and Revisons-2018 | Douglas Scott – Academia.edu. Sgt Michael P. Madden (1841–1883) – Find a Grave Memorial.

Daniel Mahoney—August 7, 1885. Pulmonary consumption and exhaustion. Died at the Barnes Hospital, Washington, D.C. https://littlebighorn.info/Cavalry/NameM.htm.

Matthew Maroney—December 15, 1880. Cause of death not stated. Interred in the Soldiers' Home National Cemetery. Matthew Maroney (1840–1880) – Find a Grave Memorial.

Michael Martin—October 5, 1877. Snake Creek, Montana. Shot in chest at Battle of Bears Paw. Nez Perce. Michael Murphy (littlebighorn.info).

George M. McDermott—September 30, 1877. Snake Creek, Montana. Battle of Bears Paw. Nez Perce. George McDermott (littlebighorn.info).

Thomas F. McLaughlin—March 3, 1886. On April 30, 1885, he was admitted to the North Dakota Hospital for the insane, where he died. He was buried in the hospital cemetery. Sgt. Thomas F. McLaughlin (1847–1886) – Find a Grave Memorial.

John McShane—April 13, 1877. Fort Abraham Lincoln. No details provided other than he was later reinterred at Custer National Cemetery.

David McWilliams—December 28,1881. Fort Meade Dakota Territory. On Sick Call during the Little Bighorn because he had been accidentally shot in the leg while hunting for the *Far West,* June 6, 1876. Cause of death—suicide by overdose of laudanum. https://www.menwithcuster.com/40/.

John Meyers—December 26, 1877. Fort Abraham Lincoln. Consumption. This Week in Little Bighorn History – Little Bighorn History (lbha.org).

Max Mielke—September 30, 1877. Snake Creek, MT. Battle with the Nez Perce. Max Mielke (littlebighorn.info).

John Mullen—August 29, 1888. Died in San Francisco. No cause of death given. https://littlebighorn.info/Cavalry/NameM.htm.

Lawrence Murphy—January 13, 1888. Soldiers' Home, Washington, D.C. No details. Lawrence Murphy (littlebighorn.info).

Thomas Murray—August 4, 1888. Congressional Medal of Honor. Died at the Soldiers' Home, Washington, D.C. Chronic bronchitis, and disabled due to an injury on February 10, 1888. Served in the Civil War. https://www.findagrave.com/memorial/6050790/thomas-murray.

John Noonan—November 30, 1878. Fort Abraham Lincoln. Committed suicide after wife's identity as a man discovered upon her death. He was on detached duty during the Little Bighorn. Seventh Cavalry – Surnames Beginning with N (littlebighorn.info).

Olans H. Northeg—November 5, 1882. Fort Meade, Dakota Territory. Suicide. https://littlebighorn.info/Cavalry/NameN.htm#Northeg.

Thomas O'Brien—September 15, 1876. Fort Buford, Dakota Territory. Typhoid fever. On detached service during the battle. https://littlebighorn.info/Cavalry/NameO.htm.

John O'Neill—March 8, 1888. Washington, D.C. No further details. John O'Neill (1848–1888) – Find a Grave Memorial.

Henry W. Raichel—September 30, 1877. Killed in the Nez Perce war. Snake Creek, Montana Territory. Henry Raichel (littlebighorn.info).

William J. Randall—September 30, 1877. Killed in the Nez Perce war. Snake Creek, Montana Territory. William Randall (littlebighorn.info).

Marcus Albert Reno—March 30, 1889. Cancer of the tongue. Erratic last years. In 1904, a story in the *Northwestern Christian Advocate* claimed that Reno had admitted to its former editor that "his strange actions" during and after the Battle of Little Bighorn were "due to drink." W. A. Graham, *The Custer Myth: A Source Book of Custeriana* (Mechanicsburg, PA: Stackpole, 2000), 338–39. Marcus Albert Reno (1834–1889) – Find a Grave Memorial.

Frances Roth—September 30, 1877. Killed in the Nez Perce war. Snake Creek, Montana Territory. Francis Roth (littlebighorn.info).

Robert Rowland—April 15, 1879. Self-inflicted gunshot wound to the head. Apparent suicide. Corp. Robert George Rowland (1843–1879) – Find a Grave Memorial.

Stephen L. Ryan—April 18, 1885. Buried in St. Mary's Cemetery, Bismarck, North Dakota. No further details. Seventh Cavalry — Surnames Beginning with R (littlebighorn.info).

William M. Shields—September 6, 1887. No further details. Middle initial possibly H. Pvt. William Hall Shields (1837–1888) – Find a Grave Memorial.

John R. Steinker—November 28, 1876. Fort Abraham Lincoln. Suicide by poison in company quarters. https://www.littlebighorn.info/Cavalry/NameS.htm#WilliamShields.

Elijah T. Strode—February 14, 1881. Shot in Miller's Saloon by Private Whalen. https://www.littlebighorn.info/Cavalry/NameS.htm #WilliamShields.

John W. Sweeney—April 14, 1884. Died in Kentucky. No further details. Seventh Cavalry – Surnames Beginning with S (littlebighorn.info).

Richard A. Wallace—July 25, 1876. Drowned crossing the Bighorn River. https://lbha.org/?tag=wallace.

George Weaver—October 14,1886. Fort Meade. No details. Pvt. George Weaver (1842–1886) – Find a Grave Memorial.

James Weeks—August 26, 1877. Shot and killed by Bernard Golden at Crow Agency. https://littlebighorn.info/Cavalry/NameW.htm #JamesWeeks. Golden also fought at the Little Bighorn.

Thomas Benton Weir—December 9, 1876. Governors Island, New York. Reportedly deeply shaken by events he had witnessed at the Little Bighorn, he began drinking heavily and his health declined. https://billingsgazette.com/news/features/magazine/haunted-by-history -tragedy-followed-bighorn-battle-survivors/article_a5fd2a85-616e-5aeb -a183-449ce45a0410.html.

Markus Weiss—November 15,1879. Death caused by cave-in of a gravel bank, resulting in a compound fracture of his neck. https://lbha.org/?tag =weiss.

William Whitlow—September 30, 1877. Killed in the Nez Perce war. Snake Creek, Montana Territory. William Whitlow (littlebighorn.info).

NOTES

1. Dorothy M. Johnson, *The Bloody Bozeman* (New York and Toronto: McGraw-Hill Book Company, 1971), 4.

INTRODUCTION

1. https://www2.census.gov/library/publications/decennial/1870/population/1870a -56.pdf?#.
2. *The Montana Post* (Virginia City), August 27, 1864, 3.
3. CPI Inflation Calculator, accessed November 12, 2022, https://www.officialdata.org /us/inflation/1910?amount=1.

CHAPTER 1

1. Michael P. Malone, Richard B. Roeder and William L. Lang, *Montana: A History of Two Centuries* (Seattle and London: University of Washington Press, 1991), 32.
2. B. Derek Strahn, *The Montana Medicine Show's Genuine Montana History* (Helena: Riverbend, 2014), 11.
3. Malone, Roeder, and Lang, *Montana: A History of Two Centuries*, 34.
4. Lewis and Clark Journals, Joseph Whitehouse entry, accessed June 29, 2020, https: //lewisandclarkjournals.unl.edu/item/lc.jrn.1805-07-04.
5. Malone, Roeder, and Lang, *Montana: A History of Two Centuries*, 38.
6. Eric Jay Dolin, *Fur, Fortune, and Empire: The Epic History of the Fur Trade in America*, (New York and London: W.W. Norton & Company, 2010), 122.
7. Dictionary of Canadian Biography, accessed November 13, 2022, http://www .biographi.ca/en/bio/mckenzie_charles_8E.html.
8. K. Ross Toole, *Montana: An Uncommon Land* (Norman: University of Oklahoma Press, 1984), 42–43.
9. "Forts and Fights of the Mountain West," accessed January 5, 2020, https://www .northamericanforts.com/West/mt3.html.
10. Three Forks Chamber of Commerce. https://threeforksmontana.com/threeforks/ history/.
11. Malone, Roeder, and Lang, *Montana: A History of Two Centuries*, 49.
12. Strahn, *The Montana Medicine Show's Genuine Montana History*, 21.

13. Kim Briggeman, *The Missoulian*, August 21, 2009, https://missoulian.com/lifestyles/territory/montana-history-almanac-brutal-fighting-breaks-out-at-fort-mckenzie/article_cb724ae2-8e80-11de-9036-001cc4c03286.html.

14. Malone, Roeder, and Lang, *Montana: A History of Two Centuries*, 57.

15. Montana Trappers Association, accessed January 5, 2020, https://www.montanatrappers.org/history/fur-posts.htm.

16. Forts and Fights of the Mountain West, accessed January 5, 2020, https://www.northamericanforts.com/West/mt3.html#koot5.

17. Fort Connah Restoration Society, accessed January 5, 2020, http://www.fortconnah.org/#intro.

18. Francis D. Haines, Jr., "The Relations of the Hudson's Bay Company with the American Fur Traders in the Pacific Northwest," *Pacific Northwest Quarterly* 40, no. 4 (October 1949): 273–94, accessed September 10, 2022, https://www.jstor.org/stable/40486851?read-now=1&refreqid=excelsior%3Ae2df27df6dc3774fba69ee4a8d0dee40&seq=22#page_scan_tab_contents.

CHAPTER 2

1. Washington Irving, *The Adventures of Captain Bonneville*, vol. 1 (Originally published 1837), 25–27.

2. Thomas James, *Three Years among the Indians and the Mexicans* (St. Louis, Missouri Historical Society, 1916), 10.

3. James, *Three Years among the Indians*, 15.

4. James, *Three Years among the Indians*, 13.

5. Michael P. Malone, Richard B. Roeder, and William L. Lang, *Montana: A History of Two Centuries* (Seattle and London: University of Washington Press, 1991), 46.

6. B. Derek Strahn, *The Montana Medicine Show's Genuine Montana History* (Helena: Riverbend, 2014), 21.

7. Eric Jay Dolin, *Fur, Fortune, and Empire: The Epic History of the Fur Trade in America* (New York and London: W.W. Norton & Company, 2010), 227.

8. Dolin, *Fur, Fortune, and Empire*, 252.

9. Strahn, *The Montana Medicine Show's Genuine Montana History*, 23.

10. James, *Three Years among the Indians*, 57.

11. "Hugh Glass Letter on Display at Cultural Heritage Center," https://history.sd.gov/archives/forms/news/2016/Hugh%20Glass%20Letter%20APPROVED.pdf.

12. Brett French, "Researcher Sets Record Straight on Famed Mountain Man Hugh Glass' Death," December 27, 2016, https://billingsgazette.com/news/state-and-regional/montana/researcher-sets-record-straight-on-famed-mountain-man-hugh-glass/article_628ca624-9c9d-596a-bf4b-89fdd97bc116.html. The researcher credited with the discovery was Clay Landry.

13. James, *Three Years among the Indians*, 80.

Chapter 3

1. Bannack Association, *Bannack* pamphlet (Dillon: Montana Fish, Wildlife & Parks and The Bannack Association, n.d.), 2.

2. Michael Malone, Richard B. Roeder, and William L. Lang, *Montana: A History of Two Centuries* (Norman: University of Oklahoma Press, 1984), 68.

3. Frederick Allen, *A Decent and Orderly Lynching* (Norman: University of Oklahoma Press, 2009), 71.

4. Granville Stuart, *Prospecting for Gold: From Dogtown to Virginia City 1852–1864* (Lincoln and London: University of Nebraska Press, 1977), 232.

5. Bannack Association, *Bannack,* 5.

6. Robert Vaughn, *Then and Now: Or Thirty-Six Years in the Rockies, Personal Reminiscences of Some of the First Pioneers of the State of Montana. Indians and Indian Wars. The Past and Present of the Rocky Mountain Country, 1864–1900* (Tribune Printing Company, 1900), 39. https://www.gutenberg.org/files/47334/47334-h/47334-h.htm#Page_39, accessed November 16, 2022.

7. K. Ross Toole, *Montana: A History of Two Centuries* (Norman: University of Oklahoma Press, 1984), 65.

8. Stuart, *Prospecting for Gold,* 263.

9. Stuart, *Prospecting for Gold,* 265.

10. Earl of Dunraven, *The Great Divide: Travels in the Upper Yellowstone in the Summer of 1874* (1876).

11. Stuart, *Prospecting for Gold,* 266.

12. Reported reminiscences of Robert Kirkpatrick in 1863. Bannack Association, *Bannack,* 4.

Chapter 4

1. Nathaniel Pitt Langford, *Vigilante Days and Ways: The Pioneers of the Rockies—The Makers and Making of Montana, Idaho, Oregon, Washington and Wyoming* (D.D. Merrill Company, 1893), 188.

2. Thomas J. Dimsdale, *The Vigilantes of Montana: Violence and Justice on the Frontier* (London: Lume Books, 2018), 27.

3. *Independent Record,* Helena, Montana, July 11, 1937, 11, accessed November 16, 2022, https://newspaperarchive.com/helena-independent-jul-11-1937-p-1/.

4. Langford, *Vigilante Days and Ways,* 188.

5. Langford, *Vigilante Days and Ways,* 120.

6. Langford, *Vigilante Days and Ways,* 121.

7. Langford, *Vigilante Days and Ways,* 137.

8. Langford, *Vigilante Days and Ways,* 176.

9. Dorothy M. Johnson, *The Bloody Bozeman* (New York and Toronto: McGraw-Hill, 1971), 92–93.

Chapter 5

1. Frederick Allen, *A Decent, Orderly Lynching: The Montana Vigilantes* (Norman: University of Oklahoma Press, 2009), 196.
2. Allen, *A Decent, Orderly Lynching*, 210.
3. Allen, *A Decent, Orderly Lynching*, 244.
4. Ibid.
5. Perry Eberhart, *Ghosts of the Colorado Plains* (Athens, OH: Swallow Press/Ohio University Press, 1986), 14.
6. Jack Slade.pdf (slcdocs.com), accessed December 9, 2022.
7. *Montana Post*, September 23, 1865, accessed May 5, 2022, https://chroniclingamerica.loc.gov/lccn/sn83025293/1865-09-23/ed-1/seq-3/.

Chapter 6

1. Marilyn J. Drew, "A Brief History of the Bozeman Trail," November 20, 2014, accessed September 10, 2022. https://www.wyohistory.org/encyclopedia/brief-history-bozeman-trail.
2. Grace Raymond Hebard and E. A. Brininstool, *The Bozeman Trail: Overland Routes into the Northwest and the Fights with Red Cloud's Warriors* (annotated), (originally published 1922; Big Byte Books, 2016), 121.
3. Hebard and Brininstool, *The Bozeman Trail*, 122.
4. Paul R. Wylie, *Blood on the Marias: The Baker Massacre* (Norman: University of Oklahoma Press, 2016), 71.
5. Wylie, *Blood on the Marias*, 71.
6. Wylie, *Blood on the Marias*, 76.
7. *The Montana Post*, February 3, 1866, accessed September 24, 2022, https://chroniclingamerica.loc.gov/lccn/sn83025293/1866-02-03/ed-1/seq-1/#date1=1866&index=18&rows=20&words=&searchType=basic&sequence=0&state=Montana&date2=1866&proxtext=&y=0&x=0&dateFilterType=yearRange&page=1.
8. Hebard and Brininstool, *The Bozeman Trail*, 124.
9. Hebard and Brininstool, *The Bozeman Trail*, 121.
10. Quote attributed to Captain William J. Fetterman in November of 1866.
11. Frank Rzeczkowski, "The Crow Indians and the Bozeman Trail," *Montana: The Magazine of Western History* 49, no. 4 (1999): 30–47. http://www.jstor.org/stable/4520184.
12. Evidence of Capt. T. Ten Eyck, 18th U.S. Infy., on the Fort Phil. Kearney Massacre, July 5, 1867, accessed September 26, 2022, https://freepages.rootsweb.com/~familyinformation/history/fpk/teneyck.html.
13. Ibid.
14. Hebard and Brininstool, *The Bozeman Trail*, 121.
15. Jerome A. Green, "The Hayfield Fight: A Reappraisal of a Neglected Action," *Montana: The Magazine of Western History* 22, no. 4 (1972): 36, http://www.jstor.org/stable/4517717.
16. Green, "The Hayfield Fight," 36.
17. Green, "The Hayfield Fight," 37.
18. Green, "The Hayfield Fight," 39.

CHAPTER 7

1. Fanny Kelly, *Narrative of My Captivity Among the Sioux Indians* (originally published 1871; Laramie Press, 2019), 137.

2. Kelly, *Narrative of My Captivity*, 60.

3. Kelly, *Narrative of My Captivity*, 7.

3. Kelly, *Narrative of My Captivity*, 7.

4. Kelly, *Narrative of My Captivity*, 21.

5. Ibid.

6. Kelly, *Narrative of My Captivity*, 26.

7. *Chicago Daily News Record*, January 10, 1880, 1.

8. *Sunday World Herald* (Omaha), March 17, 1901, 21.

9. Civil War, Battle Unit Details, Union Kansas Volunteers, accessed November 18, 2022, https://www.nps.gov/civilwar/search-battle-units-detail.htm?battleUnitCode =UKS0011RC.

10. Lieut. J. B. Goe, "The Army of the US Historical Sketches of Staff and Line with Portraits of Generals-in-Chief: Thirteenth Regiment of Infantry," US Army Center of Military History, accessed November 17, 2022, https://history.army.mil/books/r&h/R &H-13IN.htm.

11. Annette Kolodny, "Among the Indians: The Uses of Captivity," *Women's Studies Quarterly* 21, no. 3/4 (1993): 184–95, accessed November 17, 2022, http://www.jstor.org /stable/40022022, 192.

12. "Camp Cooke, Montana," Legends of America, accessed November 17, 2022, https://www.legendsofamerica.com/camp-cooke-montana/.

13. Jeremy Agnew, *Life of a Soldier on the Western Frontier* (Missoula: Mountain Press Publishing Company, 2008), 11.

14. Agnew, *Life of a Soldier*, 114.

15. Agnew, *Life of a Soldier*, 155.

CHAPTER 8

1. Paul R. Wylie, *Blood on the Marias: The Baker Massacre*. (Norman: University of Oklahoma Press. 2016), 11.

2. Wylie, *Blood on the Marias*, 33.

3. Ibid.

4. Wylie, *Blood on the Marias*, 40.

5. Kerry R. Oman, *The Beginning of the End: The Indian Peace Commission of 1867–1868*, accessed October 4, 2022, https://digitalcommons.unl.edu/cgi/viewcontent.cgi?article =3353&context=greatplainsquarterly, 37.

6. Wylie, *Blood on the Marias*, 112.

7. Wylie, *Blood on the Marias*, 114.

8. James Welch and Paul Stekler, *Killing Custer* (New York, London: W. W. Norton & Company, 1994), 27.

9. Welch and Stekler, *Killing Custer*, 29.

10. Wylie, *Blood on the Marias*, 169.

11. Wylie, *Blood on the Marias*, 177.

12. Welch and Stekler, *Killing Custer*, 31.

13. Welch and Stekler, *Killing Custer*, 33.

14. Wylie, *Blood on the Marias*, 239.

15. Wylie, *Blood on the Marias*, 243.

16. Helen B. West, "Blackfoot Country," *Montana: The Magazine of Western History* 10, no. 4 (1960): 34–44, http://www.jstor.org/stable/4516437, 43.

17. Hugh A. Dempsey, "Cypress Hills Massacre," *The Montana Magazine of History* 3, no. 4 (1953): 1–9, http://www.jstor.org/stable/4515883, 8.

18. Dempsey, "Cypress Hills Massacre," 2.

CHAPTER 9

1. "Those Who Served: The US Army on the Frontier," accessed September 20, 2022, https://nationalcowboymuseum.org/explore/served-u-s-army-frontier/.

2. "Terry's Official Report on the Custer Disaster," accessed August 31, 2022, https://littlebighorn.info/Articles/terryre1.htm.

3. Lakota Chief Red Horse's account of the Battle of the Little Bighorn given in 1881. https://www.digitalhistory.uh.edu/disp_textbook.cfm?smtID=3&psid=4023.

4. Thomas Powers, "How the Battle of Little Bighorn Was Won," November 2020, https://www.smithsonianmag.com/history/how-the-battle-of-little-bighorn-was-won-63880188/.

5. Powers, "How the Battle of Little Bighorn Was Won."

6. Walt Cross, *Custer's Lost Officer: The Search for Lieutenant Henry Moore Harrington, 7th U.S. Cavalry* (Stillwater, OK: Cross Publications, 2006), 148.

7. Douglas D. Scott, P. Willey, and Melissa A. Connor, *They Died with Custer: Soldiers' Bones from the Battle of the Little Bighorn* (Norman: University of Oklahoma Press, 2002), 97.

8. Lorna Thackeray, "Haunted by History: Tragedy Followed Bighorn Battle Survivors," accessed October 18, 2022, https://billingsgazette.com/news/features/magazine/haunted-by-history-tragedy-followed-bighorn-battle-survivors/article_a5fd2a85-616e-5aeb-a183-449ce45a0410.html

9. Albert Dr. Winkler, "Panic, Erratic Behavior, and the Psychological Impact of the Battle of the Little Bighorn on the Soldiers, Including the Swiss Troopers," *Swiss American Historical Society Review* 55, no. 2 (2019), accessed October 13, 2022, https://scholarsarchive.byu.edu/cgi/viewcontent.cgi?article=1004&context=sahs_review, 48.

10. Winkler, "Panic, Erratic Behavior," 49.

11. Winkler, "Panic, Erratic Behavior," 55.

12. Winkler, "Panic, Erratic Behavior," 68.

13. Ibid.

14. 7th US Cavalry 1876 roster, accessed November 1, 2022, https://www.friendslittlebighorn.com/7thUSCavalry1876.pdf.

15. Thackeray, "Haunted by History."

16. Harry W. Fritz, Mary J. Murphy, and Robert Swartout Jr., *Montana Legacy* (Helena, MT: Historical Society Press, 2002), 32.

17. Fritz, Murphy, and Swartout, *Montana Legacy*, 35.

18. Orin G. Libby, *Custer's Scouts at the Little Bighorn: The Arikara Narrative of the Campaign Against the Hostile Dakotas, June 1876* (originally published in 1920; Big Byte Books, 2016).

19. *Portville Review* (Cattaraugus County, NY), June 16, 1932, accessed October 18, 2022, https://www.geni.com/people/Grace-Harrington/6000000031161313257.

20. Walt Cross, *Custer's Lost Officer: The Search for Lieutenant Henry Moore Harrington, 7th U.S. Cavalry* (Walt Cross, 2006), 148.

21. Cross, *Custer's Lost Officer*, 176–83.

CHAPTER 10

1. Thomas J. Dimsdale, *The Vigilantes of Montana: Violence and Justice* (London: Lume Books, 2016), 11.

2. E. C. "Teddy Blue" Abbott and Helena Huntington Smith, *We Pointed Them North: Recollections of a Cowpuncher* (Norman: University of Oklahoma Press, 1986), 107.

3. Warren J. Brier, "Tilting Skirts & Hurdy-Gurdies: A Commentary on Gold Camp Women," *Montana: The Magazine of Western History* 19, no. 4 (1969): 67. http://www.jstor.org/stable/4517405.

4. Brier, "Tilting Skirts & Hurdy-Gurdies," 66.

5. Paula Petrik, "Capitalists with Rooms: Prostitution in Helena, Montana, 1865–1900," *Montana: The Magazine of Western History* 31, no. 2 (1981): 28–41, http://www.jstor.org/stable/4518564.

6. Lael Morgan, *Wanton West: Madams, Money, Murder and the Wild Women of Montana's Frontier* (Chicago: Chicago Review Press, 2011), 17.

7. Morgan, *Wanton West,* 18.

8. *Montana Post,* February 19, 1869, accessed September 13, 2022, https://chroniclingamerica.loc.gov/lccn/sn83025293/1869-02-19/ed-1/seq-8/ - date1=1869&sort=date&date2=1873&searchType=advanced&language=&sequence=0&lccn.

9. Ellen Baumler and Jon Axline, *Hidden History of Helena, Montana* (Charleston, SC: History Press), 50.

10. *Helena Daily Herald,* January 9, 1872.

11. *Helena Weekly Herald,* July 31, 1873.

12. *The New North-West* (Deer Lodge, MT), September 3, 1886, 3.

13. Rex C. Myers, "An Inning for Sin: Chicago Joe and Her Hurdy-Gurdy Girls Girls Girls Girls," *Montana: The Magazine of Western History* 27, no. 2 (1977): 24–33, http://www.jstor.org/stable/4518161.

14. *The Helena Independent,* July 15, 1898, 7.

15. Paula Petrik, "Capitalists with Rooms," 37.

16. Ibid.

17. Ibid.

18. Michael Zelenko, "The Tongs of China Town—Interview with Bill Lee," accessed September 19, 2022, https://www.foundsf.org/index.php?title=The_Tongs_of_Chinatown.

19. Alexy Simmons, "Red Light Ladies in the American West: Entrepreneurs and Companions," *Australian Journal of Historical Archaeology* 7 (1989): 63–69, accessed September 12, 2022, http://www.jstor.org/stable/29543241.

20. Diana L. Ahmad, *The Opium Debate and Chinese Exclusion Laws in the Nineteenth-Century American West* (Reno and Las Vegas: University of Nevada Press), 48.

21. *New Northwest* (Deer Lodge County), 1869–1888, https://hs.umt.edu/chineseinmontana/documents/TheNewNorthwest.pdf

22. A History of Montana's Early Chinese, January 31, 2016, http://www.bigskywords.com/montana-blog/a-history-of-montanas-early-chinese.

23. Mary Murphy, "The Private Lives of Public Women: Prostitution in Butte, Montana, 1878–1917," *Frontiers: A Journal of Women Studies* 7, no. 3 (1984): 30–35, doi.org/10.2307/3346238.

24. *Weekly Miner* (Butte, MT), November 4, 1879, https://chroniclingamerica.loc.gov/lccn/sn84036032/1879-11-04/ed-1/seq-5/.

25. Murphy, "The Private Lives of Public Women," 33.

CHAPTER 11

1. Meriwether Lewis and William Clark, *History of the Expedition of Captain Lewis and Clark, 1804-5-6,* vol. 1 (Chicago: AC McClurg, 1903), 332.

2. Ellen Baumler and Jon Axline, *Hidden History of Helena, Montana* (Charleston, SC: The History Press, 2019), 13.

3. *Montana Post* (Virginia City), no. 27, February 25, 1865, accessed March 13, 2022, https://chroniclingamerica.loc.gov/lccn/sn83025293/1865-02-25/ed-1/seq-1/.

4. Bob Fletcher, "Montana Medley," *The Montana Magazine of History* 3, no. 4 (1953): 50–57, http://www.jstor.org/stable/4515890.

5. Marc C. Dillon, *Montana Vigilantes, 1863–1870: Gold, Guns and Gallows* (Logan: Utah State University Press, 2013), 195.

6. *Montana Post*, September 23, 1865.

7. Dillon, *Montana Vigilantes*, 201.

8. Dillon, *Montana Vigilantes*, 207. Based on Thomas J. Dimsdale, *The Vigilantes of Montana: Violence and Justice on the Frontier*, 208.

9. Dimsdale, *Vigilantes of Montana*, 207.

10. Frederick Allen, "Montana Vigilantes and the Origins of 3-7-77," *Montana: The Magazine of Western History* 51 (Spring 2001).

11. "A Caution to the Desperate," *Montana Post*, January 5, 1867, 8.

12. Dillon, *Montana Vigilantes*, 213.

13. Dillon, *Montana Vigilantes*, 214.

14. *Montana Radiator* (Helena, Montana Territory), January 27, 1866.

15. *Montana Radiator* (Helena, Montana Territory), February 17, 1866.

16. John R. Wunder, "Law and Chinese in Frontier Montana," *Montana: The Magazine of Western History* 30, no. 3 (1980): 18–31, http://www.jstor.org/stable/4518505, 20.

17. Wunder, "Law and Chinese in Frontier Montana," 20.

18. Wunder, "Law and Chinese in Frontier Montana," 25.

19. Dillon, *Montana Vigilantes*, 215.

20. Dillon, *Montana Vigilantes*, 217.
21. Michael P. Malone, Richard B. Roeder, and William L. Lang, *Montana: A History of Two Centuries* (Seattle and London: University of Washington Press, 1991), 110.
22. "50 Facts from Montana History: # 26, *Great Falls Tribune*, October 13, 2014, accessed November 27, 2022, https://www.greatfallstribune.com/story/news/2014/10/13/50-countdown-26/17196387/.
23. W. Turrentine Jackson. "The Irish Fox and the British Lion: The Story of Tommy Cruse, the Drum Lummon, and the Montana Company, Limited (British)." *Montana: The Magazine of Western History* 9, no. 2 (1959): 28–42. http://www.jstor.org/stable/4516291.
24. Baumler and Axline, *Hidden History of Helena*, 58.
25. Malone, Roeder, and Lang, *Montana: A History of Two Centuries*, 214.

CHAPTER 12

1. "rustler," accessed December 15, 2022, https://www.etymonline.com/word/rustler#etymonline_v_48275.
2. Ernest Staples Osgood, *The Day of the Cattleman* (Chicago and London: The University of Chicago Press, 1970), 55.
3. T. A. Clay, "A Call to Order: Law, Violence and the Development of Montana's Early Stockmen's Organizations," *Montana Magazine* (Autumn 2008), 51, accessed December 15, 2022, 2602-B075-F10-001-035.pdf (montana.edu).
4. Clay, "A Call to Order," 54.
5. *Daily Enterprise*, October 24, 1884, accessed May 4, 2022, https://chroniclingamerica.loc.gov/lccn/sn85053382/1884-10-24/ed-1/seq-3/.
6. *River Press*, November 7, 1883, accessed May 4, 2022, https://chroniclingamerica.loc.gov/lccn/sn85053157/1883-11-07/ed-1/seq-3/.
7. "Lewistown's 1884 Fourth of July Shootout a Wild West Legend," *Billings Gazette*, July 4, 2010, accessed December 17, 2022. https://billingsgazette.com/news/state-and-regional/montana/lewistown-s-1884-fourth-of-july-shootout-a-wild-west-legend/article_01679dd8-871d-11df-8f74-001cc4c03286.html#tncms-source=login.
8. *Helena Weekly Herald*, July 24, 1884, 4.
9. *Sun River Sun*, August 21, 1884, 2, accessed May 5, 2022, https://chroniclingamerica.loc.gov/lccn/sn86075197/1884-08-21/ed-1/seq-2/.
10. *Kevin Review* (Kevin, MT), January 19, 1928, accessed May 5, 2022, https://chroniclingamerica.loc.gov/lccn/sn85053343/1928-01-19/ed-1/seq-7/.
11. B. Derek Strahn, *The Montana Medicine Show's Genuine Montana History* (Helena, MT: Riverbend Publishing, 2014), 87.
12. Oscar O. Mueller, "The Central Montana Vigilante Raids of 1884," *Montana Magazine of History* 1, no. 1 (1951): 23–35, http://www.jstor.org/stable/4515709, 32.
13. E. C. "Teddy Blue" Abbot and Helena Huntington Smith, *We Pointed Them North: Recollections of a Cowpuncher* (Norman: University of Oklahoma Press, 1986), 146.
14. Clay, "A Call to Order," 61.

15. Rex C. Myers, "The Fateful Numbers 3-7-77: A Re-Examination," *Montana: The Magazine of Western History* 24, no. 4 (1974): 67–70, http://www.jstor.org/stable/4517928, 69.

16. Myers, "The Fateful Numbers 3-7-77," 70.

CHAPTER 13

1. Michael P. Malone, *The Battle for Butte: Mining & Politics on the Northern Frontier 1864–1906* (Helena: Montana Historical Society Press, 1981), 7.

2. Malone, *The Battle for Butte*, 9.

3. Ibid.

4. Malone, *The Battle for Butte*, 25

5. Discover Mining History with the Mining History Association, https://www.mininghistoryassociation.org/ButteHistory.htm.

6. Brian Shovers, "The Perils of Working in the Butte Underground: Industrial Fatalities in the Copper Mines, 1880–1920," *Montana: The Magazine of Western History* 37, no. 2 (1987): 26–39. http://www.jstor.org/stable/4519048, 32.

7. Malone, *The Battle for Butte*, 57.

8. *Daily Inter Mountain* (Butte, MT), December 31, 1900, 8.

9. Shovers, "The Perils of Working in the Butte Underground," 28.

10. Ellen Baumler, "Devil's Perch: Prostitution from Suite to Cellar in Butte, Montana," *Montana: The Magazine of Western History* 48, no. 3 (1998): 4–21, http://www.jstor.org/stable/4520070.

11. Malone, *The Battle for Butte*, 74.

12. *The Butte Miner*, November 4, 1881.

13. "Doctor Huie Pock," Mai Wah Museum, accessed December 1, 2022, https://www.maiwah.org/explore/butte-chinese-experience/doctor-huie-pock/.

14. *The Butte Miner*, November 4, 1881.

15. Malone, *The Battle for Butte*, 136.

APPENDIX A

1. Fort Assinniboine, Havre, Montana, accessed September 30, 2020, https://fortassinniboine.org/about/.

2. Fort Belknap Indian Community, accessed December 30, 2022, https://ftbelknap.org/history.

3. Fort Benton Museums, Old Fort Benton, accessed December 30, 2022, http://www.fortbenton.com/fbrestore/history.html.

4. Rodger Lee Huckabee, "Camp Cooke: The First Army Post in Montana—Success and Failure on the Missouri," Boise State University Theses and Dissertations, August 2010, 153. https://scholarworks.boisestate.edu/td/153.

5. "Six Crow Scouts outside Fort Custer, Late 19th Century," Distinctly Montana, accessed December 30, 2022, https://www.distinctlymontana.com/six-crow-scouts-outside-fort-custer-late-19th-century.

6. Legends of America, accessed December 30, 2022, https://www.legendsofamerica .com/fort-elizabeth-meagher-montana/.

7. Legends of America, https://www.legendsofamerica.com/fort-ellis-montana/.

8. Legends of America, accessed December 30, 2022, https://www.legendsofamerica .com/fort-keogh-montana/.

9. Library of Congress, accessed December 30, 2022, https://www.loc.gov/resource/ hhh.mt0029.photos?st=gallery.

10. Enjoy Lewistown, accessed December 30, 2022, https://www.enjoylewistown.com /fort-maginnis.

11. Historical Museum at Fort Missoula, accessed September 5, 2022, https:// fortmissoulamuseum.org/history/.

12. Fort Parker, the First Crow Indian Agency, accessed September 5, 2022, https:// fortparkerhistory.org.

13. Legends of America, accessed September 5, 2022, https://www.legendsofamerica .com/fort-shaw-montana.

14. E. M. Richardson, "The Forgotten Haycutters at Fort C. F. Smith," *Montana: The Magazine of Western History* 9, no. 3 (1959): 22–33, http://www.jstor.org/stable/4516306.

REFERENCES

BOOKS

Abbot, E. C. "Teddy Blue." *We Pointed Them North: Recollections of a Cowpuncher*. Norman: University of Oklahoma Press, 1986.

Agnew, Jeremy. *Life of a Soldier on the Western Frontier*. Missoula, MT: Mountain Press Publishing Company, 2008.

Ahmad, Diana L. *The Opium Debate and Chinese Exclusion Laws in the Nineteenth-Century American West*. Reno and Las Vegas: University of Nevada Press, 2007.

Allen, Frederick. *A Decent and Orderly Lynching*. Norman: University of Oklahoma Press, 2009.

Bannack Association, Bannack pamphlet. Dillon, MT: Fish, Wildlife & Parks with the Bannack Association, date unknown.

Baumler, Ellen, and Jon Axline. *Hidden History of Helena, Montana*. Charleston, SC: History Press, 2019.

Beckwourth, James Pierson. *The Life and Adventures of James P. Beckwourth: Mountaineer, Scout, and Pioneer, and Chief of the Crow Nation of Indians*. Harper Brothers, 1856. Citations refer to 2016 edition.

Bradley, James Howard. *The March of the Montana Column: A Prelude to the Custer Disaster*. Norman: University of Oklahoma Press, 1961.

Butler, Anne M. *Daughters of Joy, Sisters of Misery: Prostitutes in the American West, 1865–90*. Urbana and Chicago: University of Illinois Press, 1985.

Collins, Jan MacKell. *Good Time Girls of the Rocky Mountains: A Red-Light History of Montana, Idaho and Wyoming*. Guilford, CT: TwoDot, 2020.

Cooke, Phillip St. George. *Some True Adventures in the Life of Hugh Glass, a Hunter and Trapper on the Missouri River* (1857). Publisher unknown.

Cross, Walt. *Custer's Lost Officer: The Search for Lieutenant Henry Moore Harrington, 7th U.S. Cavalry*. Stillwater, OK: Cross Publications, 2006.

DeFelice, Jim. *West Like Lightning: The Brief, Legendary Ride of the Pony Express*. New York: William Morrow, 2018.

Dillon, Mark C. *Montana Vigilantes, 1863–1870: Gold, Guns, and Gallows*. Logan: Utah State University Press, 2013.

Dimsdale, Thomas J. *The Vigilantes of Montana*. London: Lume Books, 2018. Originally published by State Publishing Co., 1920.

Dolin, Eric Jay. *Fur, Fortune, and Empire: The Epic History of the Fur Trade in America*. New York and London: W.W. Norton & Company, 2010.

Gard, Wayne. *Frontier Justice*. Norman: University of Oklahoma Press, 1949.

Hamilton, William Thomas. *My Sixty Years on the Plains Trapping, Trading and Indian Fighting*. Enhanced Media, 2017. Originally published 1905.

Hebard, Grace Raymond, and Earl Alonzo Brininstool. *The Bozeman Trail*. vol. 2. Cleveland: The Arthur H. Clark Company, 1922.

Herndon, Sarah Raymond. *Days on the Road: Crossing the Plains in 1865*. London: Lume Books, 2018. Originally published 1902.

Irving, Washington. *The Adventures of Captain Bonneville, U.S.A., in the Rocky Mountains and the Far West*. Originally published 1837.

James, Thomas. *Three Years among the Indians and the Mexicans*. St. Louis: Missouri Historical Society, 1916.

Johnson, Dorothy M. *The Bloody Bozeman*. New York and Toronto: McGraw-Hill Book Company, 1971.

Kelly, Fanny. *Narrative of My Captivity Among the Sioux Indians* (1871). Kindle Version.

Langford, Nathaniel Pitt. *Vigilante Days and Ways: The Pioneers of the Rockies—The Makers and Making of Montana, Idaho, Oregon, Washington and Wyoming*. D.D. Merrill Company, 1893.

Larimer, Sarah L. *The Capture and Escape of Sarah Larimer*. Timeless Classics, 2019. Originally published 1870.

Lawrence, Jennifer J. *Soap Suds Row: The Bold Lives of Army Laundresses, 1802–1876*. Glendo, WY: High Plains Press, 2016.

Lewis, Nathan. *Gold: The Once and Future Money*. Hoboken, NJ: John Wiley & Sons, Inc, 2007.

Libby, Orin G. *Custer's Scouts at the Little Bighorn: The Arikara Narrative of the Campaign Against the Hostile Dakotas*. Big Byte Books, 2016. Originally published 1920.

Malone, Michael P., Richard B. Roeder, and William L. Lang. *Montana: A History of Two Centuries*. Seattle and London: University of Washington Press, 1991.

McCord, Monty. *Calling the Brands: Stock Detectives in the Wild West*. Guilford, CT: TwoDot, 2018.

Michno, Gregory, and Susan Michno. *A Fate Worse Than Death: Indian Captivities in the West, 1830–1885*. Caldwell, ID: Caxton Press, 2009.

Milner, Clyde A. II, and Carol A. O'Connor. *As Big as the West: The Pioneer Life of Granville Stuart*. Oxford: Oxford University Press, 2009.

Morgan, Lael. *Wanton West: Madams, Money, Murder and the Wild Women of Montana's Frontier*. Chicago: Chicago Review Press, 2011.

Osgood, Ernest Staples. *The Day of the Cattlemen*. Chicago: University of Chicago Press, 1970.

Punke, Michael. *Fire and Brimstone: The North Butte Mining Disaster of 1917*. New York: Hyperion, 2006.

Scott, Douglas D., P. Willey, and Melissa A. Connor. *They Died with Custer: Soldiers' Bones from the Battle of the Little Bighorn*. Norman: University of Oklahoma Press. 1998.

Strahn, B. Derek. *The Montana Medicine Show's Genuine Montana History*. Helena, MT: Riverbend, 2014.

Stuart, Granville. *Prospecting for Gold: From Dogtown to Virginia City 1852–1864*. Lincoln and London: University of Nebraska Press, 1977.

Taylor, William O. *With Custer on the Little Bighorn*. New York and London: Viking Penguin, 1996.

Toole, K. Ross. *Montana: An Uncommon Land*. Norman: University of Oklahoma Press, 1984.

Vaughn, Robert. *Then and Now: Or Thirty-Six Years in the Rockies, Personal Reminiscences of Some of the First Pioneers of the State of Montana. Indians and Indian Wars. The Past and Present of the Rocky Mountain Country. 1864–1900*. Tribune Printing Company, 1900.

Vickers, Marques. *The Red-Light District of Butte Montana: The Decadence and Dissolution of a Local Institution*. Herron Island, WA: Marquis Publishing, 2017.

Welch, James, and Paul Stekler. *Killing Custer*. New York, London: W. W. Norton & Company, 1994.

Willey, P. and Douglas D. Scott. *Health of the Seventh Cavalry: A Medical History*. Norman: University of Oklahoma Press, 2015.

Wylie, Paul R. *Blood on the Marias: The Baker Massacre*. Norman: University of Oklahoma Press. 2016.

Online Sources

Big Sky Words. Accessed December 5, 2022. http://www.bigskywords.com/montana-blog/a-history-of-montanas-early-chinese.

Dictionary of Canadian Biography. McKenzie, Charles. Accessed November 13, 2022. http://www.biographi.ca/en/bio/mckenzie_charles_8E.html.

Distinctly Montana. Accessed December 30, 2022. "Six Crow Scouts outside Fort Custer, Late 19th Century." (https://www.distinctlymontana.com/).

Enjoy Lewistown. Accessed December 30, 2022. Fort Maginnis. (https://www.enjoylewistown.com/).

Etymonline. Accessed December 15, 2022. rustle | Etymology, origin and meaning of *rustle* by etymonline.

Fort Assinniboine, Havre, Montana. Accessed September 30, 2020. https://fortassinniboine.org/about/.

Fort Belknap Indian Community. Accessed September 30, 2020. https://ftbelknap.org/history.

Fort Benton Museums—Old Fort Benton. Accessed September 30, 2020. http://www.fortbenton.com/fbrestore/history.html

Fort Connah Restoration Society. Accessed January 5, 2020. http://www.fortconnah.org/#intro.

Forts and Fights of the Mountain West. Accessed January 5, 2020. https://www.northamericanforts.com/West/mt3.html.

Historical Museum at Fort Missoula. Accessed September 5, 2022. https://fortmissoulamuseum.org/history/.

History South Dakota Government. Accessed February 10, 2020. https://history.sd.gov/archives/forms/news/2016/Hugh Glass Letter APPROVED.pdf.

Journals of the Lewis and Clark Expedition. Accessed January 6, 2020. https://lewisandclarkjournals.unl.edu/item/lc.jrn.1805-07-04.

Legends of America. Accessed November 17, 2022. https://legendsofamerica.com.

Library of Congress. https://loc.gov.

Mai Wah Museum, Doctor Huie Pock. Doctor Huie Pock – Mai Wah Society.

Mining History Association. https://www.mininghistoryassociation.org/ButteHistory.htm.

Montana Stockgrowers Association. (montanacowboyfame.org).

MontanaTrappers.org. https://www.montanatrappers.org/history/fur-posts.htm. Accessed January 5, 2020.

National Park Service. Accessed November 18, 2022. Battle Unit Details—The Civil War (U.S. National Park Service) (nps.gov).

National Park Service. Accessed November 2, 2022. Hayfield Fight - Bighorn Canyon National Recreation Area (U.S. National Park Service) (nps.gov).

Official Data.org. https://www.officialdata.org/us/inflation/1910?amount=1.

Salt Lake City Doc. Accessed December 9, 2022. Jack Slade.pdf (slcdocs.com).

Thirteenth Regiment of Infantry. The Army of the US Historical Sketches of Staff and Line with Portraits of Generals-in-Chief. U.S. Army Center of Military History. Accessed November 17, 2022. https://history.army.mil/books/r&h/R&H-13IN.htm.

Three Forks Chamber of Commerce. https://threeforksmontana.com/threeforks/history/.

United States Census.
    https://www2.census.gov/library/publications/decennial/1870/population/1870a-08.pdf#.
    https://www2.census.gov/library/publications/decennial/1870/population/1870a-55.pdf?#.
    https://www2.census.gov/library/publications/decennial/1870/population/1870a-56.pdf?#.

University of Montana. https://hs.umt.edu/chineseinmontana/documents/TheNew Northwest.pdf.

Wyoming History. Accessed September 10, 2022. https://www.wyohistory.org/encyclopedia.

NEWSPAPERS

Billings Gazette
Chicago Daily News Herald
Daily Enterprise
Great Falls Tribune
Helena Daily Herald
Helena Independent
Helena Weekly Herald
Independent Record (Helena)

Kevin Review (Kevin, Montana)
Missoulian
Montana Post (Virginia City)
Montana Radiator (Helena)
New North West (Deer Lodge, Montana)
River Press (Fort Benton, Montana)
Sunday World Herald (Omaha, Nebraska)
Sun River Sun (Sun River, Montana)
Weekly Miner (Butte, Montana)

JOURNAL ARTICLES

Arata, Laura J. "Terror and Tourism: Lynching, Legend, and the Montana Vigilantes." *The* Pacific *Northwest Quarterly* 106, no. 4 (2015): 183–98. http://www.jstor.org/stable/44790728.

Athearn, Robert G. "General Sherman and the Montana Frontier." *The Montana Magazine of History* 3, no. 1 (1953): 55–64. http://www.jstor.org/stable/4515838.

Baumler, Ellen. "Devil's Perch: Prostitution from Suite to Cellar in Butte, Montana." *Montana: The Magazine of Western History* 48, no. 3 (1998): 4–21. http://www.jstor.org/stable/4520070.

Brier, Warren J., "Tilting Skirts & Hurdy-Gurdies: A Commentary on Gold Camp Women." *Montana: The Magazine of Western History* 19, no. 4 (1969): 67. http://www.jstor.org/stable/4517405.

Briggeman, Kim. "Montana History Almanac: Brutal Fighting Breaks Out at Fort McKenzie." *The Missoulian* (August 21, 2009). https://missoulian.com/lifestyles/territory/montana-history-almanac-brutal-fighting-breaks-out-at-fort-mckenzie/article_cb724ae2-8e80-11de-9036-001cc4c03286.html.

Clay, T. A. "A Call to Order: Law, Violence and the Development of Montana's Early Stockmen's Organizations." *Montana Magazine*, Autumn 2008, 51. Accessed December 15, 2022. 2602-B075-F10-001-035.pdf (montana.edu).

Dempsey, Hugh A. "Cypress Hills Massacre." *The Montana Magazine of History* 3, no. 4 (1953): 1–9. http://www.jstor.org/stable/4515883.

Dempsey, Hugh A. "Howell Harris and the Whiskey Trade." *The Montana Magazine of History* 3, no. 2 (1953): 1–8. http://www.jstor.org/stable/4515851.

Eichengreen, Barry, and Ian W. McLean. "The Supply of Gold under the Pre-1914 Gold Standard." *The Economic History Review* 47, no. 2 (1994): 288–309. https://doi.org/10.2307/2598083.

Fletcher, Bob. "Montana Medley." *The Montana Magazine of History* 3, no. 4 (1953): 50–57. http://www.jstor.org/stable/4515890.

French, Brett. "Researcher Sets Record Straight on Famed Mountain Man Hugh Glass' Death." *Billings Gazette* (December 27, 2016). https://billingsgazette.com/news/state-and-.%20try%20fur,%20fortune%20etc.regional/montana/researcher-sets-record-straight-on-famed-mountain-man-hugh-glass/article_628ca624-9c9d-596a-bf4b-89fdd97bc116.html.

Green, Jerome A. "The Hayfield Fight: A Reappraisal of a Neglected Action." *Montana: The Magazine of Western History* 22, no. 4 (1972): 36. http://www.jstor.org/stable/4517717.

Haines, Francis D., Jr. "The Relations of the Hudson's Bay Company with the American Fur Traders in the Pacific Northwest." *Pacific Northwest Quarterly* 40, no. 4 (October 1949): 273–94. https://www.jstor.org/stable/40486851.

Huckabee, Rodger Lee. "Camp Cooke: The First Army Post in Montana—Success and Failure on the Missouri" (2010). Boise State University Theses and Dissertations.

Jackson, W. Turrentine. "The Irish Fox and the British Lion: The Story of Tommy Cruse, the Drum Lummon, and the Montana Company, Limited (British)." *Montana: The Magazine of Western History* 9, no. 2 (1959).

Kittredge, William, and Steven M. Krauzer. "'Mr. Montana' Revised: Another Look at Granville Stuart." *Montana: The Magazine of Western History* 36, no. 4 (1986): 14–23. http://www.jstor.org/stable/4519007.

Kolodny, Annette. "Among the Indians: The Uses of Captivity." *Women's Studies Quarterly* 21, no. 3/4 (1993): 184–95. http://www.jstor.org/stable/40022022.

Malone, Michael P., and Richard B. Roeder. "1876 in Montana: Anxiety and Anticipation." *Montana: The Magazine of Western History* 25, no. 1 (1975): 2–13. http://www.jstor.org/stable/4517953.

McGinnis, Anthony. "Strike & Retreat: Intertribal Warfare and the Powder River War, 1865–1868." *Montana: The Magazine of Western History* 30, no. 4 (1980): 30–41. http://www.jstor.org/stable/4518527.

"Montana Copper." *Montana: The Magazine of Western History* 14, no. 3 (1964): 56–61. http://www.jstor.org/stable/4516851.

Mueller, Oscar O. "The Central Montana Vigilante Raids of 1884." *The Montana Magazine of History* 1, no. 1 (1951): 23–35. http://www.jstor.org/stable/4515709.

Murphy, Mary. "The Private Lives of Public Women: Prostitution in Butte, Montana, 1878–1917." *Frontiers: A Journal of Women Studies* 7, no. 3 (1984): 30–35. Accessed September 18, 2022. https://doi.org/10.2307/3346238.

Myers, Rex C. "The Fateful Numbers 3-7-77: A Re-Examination." *Montana: The Magazine of Western History* 24, no. 4 (1974): 67–70. http://www.jstor.org/stable/4517928.

Oman, Kerry R. *The Beginning of the End: The Indian Peace Commission of 1867–1868*. Accessed October 4, 2022. https://digitalcommons.unl.edu/cgi/viewcontent.cgi?article=3353&context=greatplainsquarterly.

Petrik, Paula. "Capitalists with Rooms: Prostitution in Helena, Montana, 1865–1900." *Montana: The Magazine of Western History* 31, no. 2 (1981): 28–41. http://www.jstor.org/stable/4518564.

Richardson, E. M. "The Forgotten Haycutters at Fort C. F. Smith." *Montana: The Magazine of Western History* 9, no. 3 (1959): 22–33. http://www.jstor.org/stable/4516306.

Rzeczkowski, Frank. "The Crow Indians and the Bozeman Trail." *Montana: The Magazine of Western History* 49, no. 4 (1999): 30–47. http://www.jstor.org/stable/4520184.

Shovers, Brian. "The Perils of Working in the Butte Underground: Industrial Fatalities in the Copper Mines, 1880–1920." *Montana: The Magazine of Western History* 37, no. 2 (1987): 26–39. http://www.jstor.org/stable/4519048.

Simmons, Alexy. "Red Light Ladies in the American West: Entrepreneurs and Companions." *Australian Journal of Historical Archaeology* 7 (1989): 63–69. Accessed September 12, 2022. http://www.jstor.org/stable/29543241.

West, Helen B. "Blackfoot Country." *Montana: The Magazine of Western History* 10, no. 4 (1960): 34–44. http://www.jstor.org/stable/4516437.

Wunder, John R. "Law and Chinese in Frontier Montana." *Montana: The Magazine of Western History* 30, no. 3 (1980): 18–31. http://www.jstor.org/stable/4518505.

Zelenko, Michael. "The Tongs of China Town: A Conversation with Bill Lee." Accessed September 19, 2022. https://www.foundsf.org/index.php?title=The_Tongs_of _Chinatown.

INDEX

during, 113–14; statistics,
112–15; survivors of, 177–83
Battle of Killdeer Mountain, 82
Battle of the Big Hole, 176
Battle of the Marias (Marias
massacre), 90, 93, 95–100, *99*
Beal, Mayor, 168
Bear Head, 95
beaver pelts. *See* fur trade; fur
trade and trappers
Beckwith, Jennings, 30
Beckwourth, James, 29
Beidler, John X., 54–55, 134, 140
Bell, James M., 108
Bell, Mrs., 108–9
Bell, William H., 156
Belle, Ranche, 118
Beni, Jules, 58
Benser, John, 140
Benteen, Frederick, 104, 105,
109–10
Berg, Ole, 147
Berkeley Pit, 165–66
bicultural marriages, 11, 20–21,
22–23, 61–62
Big Elk, 20–21
Big Hole Battle engagement, 175
Big Horn River, 10
Bilboa, Tim, 161
Bissell (physician), 49
Bisshiilannuusaao, 175
Bitterroot Mountains, 6
Bitterroot Valley, 5
Bitzer, John R., 139–40
Black Elk, 106–7

Blackfeet, 7, 10, 11, 12–13, 22,
25–26, 68, 94–100, 113
Blackfeet Sioux, 83
Blackfoot Nation, 68, 69–75, 176
Black Kettle, 65–66
Blood Piegan, 68
Bloody Knife, 111
Blue Range (brothel), 167
Bozeman, John, 62–64, 73–74,
95, 174
Bozeman Trail, 62–67, *63, 65,*
70–77, 86–88, 176
Bradbury, John, 26
Bradley, Charles, 77
Bradley, James H., 81n
Bradley, Luther P., 74–75, 76–77
Brant, Abram B., 177
Braun, Frank, 112
Bridger, Jim or "Bridges," 25,
28, 64
Bridger Pass, 174
"brigades" of trappers, 20
Brings Plenty, 82, 83, 108
Brininstool, E. A., 65
Brown, Alexander, 177
Brown, George, 55
Browne, F. V., 162
Bryan, Electa, 46, 48
buffalo robes, 93
buffalo soldiers, 174
Burr, Eugene, 153
Burrows, Captain, 77
Butte, *149, 152,* 157–67; Chinese
community in, 164, 165, 167–
69; demographics of, 162–63,

fur trade and trappers, 17–30;
about, 8, 17–21, 22, 23–24;
early history of, x, 8–10; end of,
30, 86; idealization and legends
of, 17, 24, 25–30; Lewis and
Clark expedition and, 2, 8, 9;
Native peoples as trappers,
21–22; "opening" of western US
and, 15–16, 30; outposts for, 8,
10–15, 30, 86; rendezvous of,
23; as smallpox spreader, 25;
tribal marriages as alliances for,
20–21, 22–23; whiskey in trade,
92–94

Gall, 106
Gallagher, Jack, 49, 50, 55, 57
Gallatin River, 5
Gannon, Joseph, 162
Gannon, Peter, 179
Gardiner, John S., 27
Gass, Patrick, 4, 7
George, William Montell, 179
Gibbon, John, 175–76
Giessner, Annie, 122
Glass, Hugh, 25, 26–28
gold rush; in Alder Gulch, 37;
in Bannack, 31–35, *32*, 37;
in Butte, 157–58; civilization
and cost of living, 34, 37–39;
deserters and, 91; government
protection of forts and, 86–87;
in Helena, 130–32, 141–42; law
and disorder during, xii–xiii,
33–35, 39–40, *40*, 70, 130–32,

141–42; on plains of Montana,
62–64; price comparisons of
gold, xii–xiii
Gong Sing, 168
Goones, J. L., 135
Gordon, Fanny Wiggins Kelly, 84
Gordon, Johnny, 136–37
Gordon, William F., 84
Graham, Donald, 101
Graham, Mollie, 122
Grannis, John, 57
Grasshopper Creek, 31
Graves, "Whiskey Bill," 45
The Great Divide (Dunraven), 39
Great Falls, 7
Great Northern Trail, 100–101
Green, Governor, 94
grizzly bear encounter, 27–28
Gros Ventres, 68
guerilla warfare, 102–10, *103*
Guezals, Julian, 137

Haggin, James Ben Ali, 159, 170
Haiti, 2
Hankins, Al, 120, 121
Hardie, James A., 96
Harrington, Grace Allison, 114
Harrington, Grace Berard, 114
Harrington, Henry, 105, 108, 111,
114–15
Harris, William M., 179
Harvey, Alexander, 12–13
Harvey Primeau and Company, 13
Hauser, Samuel T., 52–53, 158
Hayfield Fight, 71–72, 75–77, 176

Steele, Dr., 49
Steinbrenner, John, 124
Steinker, John R., 183
Sternberg, Lieutenant, 75–76
Stevens, S., 139
Stewart, Granville, 61
Stinson, Buck, 45, 49–50, 54–55
Stone, Blanche, 162
Strasser, W. A., 162
"Stringer Jack," 151–53
Strode, Elijah T., 183
Stuart, Granville, 34, 36, 37–39,
    58, 148, 149, 151, 153, 154
Stuart, James, 36, 62
"Stuart's Stranglers," 151–53
Sturgis, Lieutenant, 105
Sullivan, Peter, 161
Sully, Alfred, 82, 83, 98
Sweeney, John W., 183
Sweeney, Mike, 36–37
Swendeman, S. X., 150–151
syphilis, 108, 111

Taylor, Noah, 80, 81
Tbalt, Nicholas, 45, 53
Telegraph lines, 70–71
Ten Eyck, Tenodore, 72–73
Territorial Capital, 140–42
Territorial Stock Association, 146
territorial veterinary surgeon, 154
Terry, Alfred, 175
Terry, General, 102–5
Teton Sioux, 113
Tevis, Lloyd, 159
The Far West (steamer), 110

Thomas lode, 161
Thompson, David, 14
3-7-77, 155–56
Three Forks Post, 11, 17–18, 29
Tiebalt, Nicholas, 45, 53
Tilden, Henry, 44
Tong, 125
Totten, Justice, 122
trading posts, 8, 10–15, 30, 86
Travelers' Rest, 6
Treaty of Fort Laramie
    (1851), 176
Treaty of Paris (1783), 9
tribal marriages as alliances, 11,
    20–21, 22–23, 61–62
Trimble, William, 156
Tuft, James, 95
Tullock, Samuel, 11, 13
Twain, Mark, 58
Two Moon, 106
typhus, 89

Union Fur Company, 14
Union Pacific Railroad, 71,
    77, 159
unions, 161, 169–70
Upham, Hiram D., 69
Uphaw, *65*
Upson, Gad, 69

Varley, John, 137
Varnum, Lieutenant, 105
Vedder, John, 46, 50–51
Vedder, Lucy, 50–51

Vigilance Committee of Bannack, 45, 53, 54–60
vigilantes, 41–43
vigilantism; background, 41–44; in Bannack, 45, 53, 54–60; in Butte, 165, 170; code of, 155–56; in Helena, *131*, 132–37, 139–40; Red Cloud's War and, 69; stock rustling and, 147–54, 155–56
Virginia City; Bozeman Trail and, 62, 64; gold rush in, 35–36, 37–40, *40*; outlaws and justice in, 49, 55–57, *56*; prostitution in, *40*, 116–18; as Territorial seat, 140, 141
Virginia Dale stage, 59
voyageurs, 9

Wade, Hattie, 123
Wagner, "Dutch John," 45
Wakefield, Gardner, 80, 81
Wallace, Richard A., 183
War Club, 114–15
"Wash," Stapleton, 49
washerwomen, 88–89, 137–39
Weeks, James, 183
Weinsheimer, William "Willie," 124
Weir, Thomas Benton, 183
Weiss, Markus, 183
Welch, Molly "Mary," 118–23, *119*
Western Federation of Miners, 169

Wheaton, Frank, 68
Wheeler, William F., 96
Which Way, *65*
whiskey, xii, 35, 39–40, 57, 59–60, 90
whiskey trade, 92–101; fur trade and, 92–95; Marias massacre and, 93, 95–100, *99*; Whoop-Up Trail and, 100–101
White, John, 31
White Chief, *79*
Whitlow, William, 183
Whoop-Up Trail, 100–101
Williams posse, 55
Wilson, Billy, 136
Wilson, Joseph, *131*, 140
Wolf, D. E., 105
wolfers, 101
Wood, George, 133–34
Wood, Maria, 4
Woolford (murder victim), 162
World War I, 161
Wright, George, 94
Wright, Sheriff, 46

Yankton, 113
Yanktonai Sioux, 113
Yates, Captain, 105
Yeager, Red, 55
Yechela, 81
You Kim, 167–68

Zachary, Bob, 45